Waiting for the Promised Man

Manna for Single Wives-in-Waiting

Other relationship-centered books by
Tiffany Buckner include:

How and Why You Should Wait on God for
Your Husband

Sex, Lies & Soul Ties

Wise Her Still

Wise Her Still Too (Volumes I and II)

Snare: When the Adulteress Hunts

Shattered Vessels: God's Way of Dealing
with an Adulterous Husband

Christian and Married: How to be One
Without Losing the Other

Christian Advice From His Wife to Her
Husband

Christian Advice From One Wife to Another

Waiting for the Promised Man

Manna for Single Wives-in-Waiting

Tiffany Buckner

www.AnointedFireHouse.com

Waiting for the Promised Man
Manna for Single Wives-in-Waiting
Copyright © 2015
Author Tiffany Buckner
Email: info@anointedfire.com

Publisher: Anointed Fire™ House
Publisher's Website: www.anointedfirehouse.com

ISBN-13: 978-0692603031
ISBN-10: 0692603034

Disclaimer: This book is designed to provide information and motivation to our readers. It is sold with the understanding that the publisher is not engaged to render any type of psychological, legal, or any other kind of professional advice. No warranties or guarantees are expressed or implied by the author, since every man has his own measure of faith. The individual author(s) shall not be liable for any physical, psychological, emotional, financial, or commercial damages, including; but not limited to, special, incidental, consequential or other damages. Our views and rights are the same: You are responsible for your own choices, actions, and results.

I dedicate this book to the many women of God who've dedicated their hearts and minds to God... the women who are more than just women-in-waiting; they are wives-in-waiting.

Table of Contents

Introduction

God gave me two powerful terms to share with you in this book: women-in-waiting and wives-in-waiting. Of course, He differentiated between the two and He told me why so many of His daughters stay in the wildernesses of their waits for so long. They haven't fully submitted themselves to Him yet. This is because many women-in-waiting lack the knowledge and the understanding they need to successfully complete their waits.

In this revelatory book, you will come to understand the difference between a woman and a wife (in God's eyes). Additionally, you will learn the difference between waiting and preparing. Your understanding of each term will help you to better position yourself to receive instructions from God throughout every season of your life. This will also help you to understand where you are with God and what you need to do to position yourself to be found by the promised man.

Get to know the rhythm of God's heartbeat so that you can better understand His plans for you. At the same time, getting to know God helps you to unlock the secrets about yourself that God has hidden in you... secrets He will not reveal until you're in full submission to Him.

This powerful book will answer many of the questions you've had regarding the wait and help to strengthen you as you prepare yourself for the man of God who is ordained to someday call you his wife.

What It Means to Be Hidden

You will hear a lot of single Christian women saying that they are hidden, meaning, they are properly aligned with the will and Word of God to be found by their God-appointed husbands. Nevertheless, the truth is that the average woman does not know what it means to be hidden. Of course, this means that the average woman is not hidden. Instead, a lot of women are what I like to refer to as religious parakeets. They say what they've heard others say, hoping that their words will mask their lack of faith and produce the very blessings they've been praying for. Nevertheless, if asked what it means to be hidden, the average woman would have to stop what she was doing and try to think up a reasonable-sounding answer. That's because we often hear things that sound right, and then, we incorporate those words or phrases into our religious vocabularies without having true revelation of what we're saying.

What exactly does it mean to be hidden in the Lord? The answer is simple: It means that God has concealed who you are to protect you from being pursued by the wrong man. The average woman in hiding has been pursued by the wrong man, so how is this statement true? The truth is that God does not conceal, or better yet, hide us from Satan's sons; He hides us from His sons.

God knows that what He has placed in the average single wife-in-waiting is so attractive that the average single man of God would pursue her if he saw her inner beauty. If he knew how anointed she was or how loving she was, he would unintentionally rise against the will of God to pursue her because faithful women in waiting are a rare commodity. Why doesn't God hide His daughters from Satan's sons? Because He has given us the spirit of wisdom, and with the spirit of wisdom comes discernment. This means that He has given us the ability to differentiate the sons of darkness from the sons of God. When a saved woman gives herself over to an unsaved man, she isn't deceived by the man; she has intentionally deceived herself because she did not believe God in regards to relationships and life. God told us not to be unequally yoked with unbelievers, but she didn't believe that doing so was a problem. God told us that darkness has no communion with light, but she didn't believe Him, so she went into the darkness and tried to lead some lost soul out with the flickering light of her faith. The problem wasn't that some man came along and persuaded her into dating or courting him;

the problem was that she did not believe
God. She was not yet convinced in regards
to the Word of God, and her lack of faith
left her open for attack. Make no mistake
about it: the wrong man is an attack against
your person, your ministry, your peace,
your finances, your health, your family and
all that is assigned to you by God.

When God hides His daughters, He is not
hiding what's evident about them, but more
so, what's not seen by carnal eyes.
Nevertheless, men walking in the fullness of
God can see the anointing on these women,
and because of this, many of their Christian
brethren would pursue them if they could
see them in the realm of the spirit. That's
why a lot of Christian women get
overlooked by their brethren in the Lord
and are often passed up for their not-so-
holy sisters. God will hide a woman's
identity, gifting and anointing from the men
who are walking in the light of Christ so that

4

she is not pursued by them. That's because most women (in the Lord) are assigned to certain men (in the Lord), and any of the relationships they enter outside of the marriages God has ordained them to enter are relationships built on and for the flesh, and would, therefore, serve as strongholds. Simply put, God doesn't want two of His own children to hinder one another, so He hides His daughters in plain sight. Some women go to churches full of single men in waiting, but they are often overlooked. This isn't because all of the men are in error; the issue is that God knows the value of the treasure He's put in the women He has declared to be wives-in-waiting. It's similar to leaving a huge, unguarded diamond on the altar at the church. Even though the men in the congregation may be good, godly men, not all of them are where they should be in the Lord. Because of this, that diamond would be stolen by a man who thinks he's entitled to it. So, to guard

the women of God, the Lord hides their
inner beauty, or better yet, the beauty that
attracts husbands to wives. External beauty
attracts men to women, but the beauty of
holiness attracts husbands to wives. Most
men who fear the Lord can tell you about
women who've been members of their
churches, but somehow, they were not
interested in those women. They didn't
recognize the beauty or value of those
women until they had been found by their
God-purposed husbands and covered by
the seal of marriage. Of course, many of
them don't understand how the women in
question slipped through their fingers, but
the truth is that the women were simply
hidden.

Men, on the other hand, don't have to be
hidden; they have to simply walk in
authority against the Devil. A man's seal of
protection is his submission to God (just like
a woman) and the way in which he is

designed. Men, by default, are hunters who only appreciate what they've had to work for. Easy kill equals easy. Anything a man hasn't worked for, he cannot and will not value, respect or appreciate. For example, if a rabbit hopped through a hunter's backyard, and that hunter lived in an area where he could shoot, kill and bag his prey, that rabbit would be considered an easy kill. The hunter didn't have to leave the comforts of his yard to catch or kill his prey. He didn't have to put on his hunter's gear or prepare his mind for the hunt. The rabbit came to him, so he'll simply go outside, kill it, skin and clean it, and then, cook it. That's it. After that, the rabbit's carcass will be discarded and the rabbit will be nothing more than just another story to tell. A hunter has to come outside his comfort zone to appreciate the kill. Of course, your man of God won't kill you, but he will appreciate the fact that he had to come outside his comfort zone to get you. His mind had to be changed and he had to be clothed in the garments of righteousness before God released you to be found by him.

There are many men out there who think they're ready to be husbands, but they aren't. Their desires to get married are centered around themselves and their own selfish ambitions, and because of this, when such men marry, they often divorce their wives within one to five years. That's because they wanted the perks of marriage without the responsibilities of marriage. It's similar to a woman seeing another woman with a child, and after admiring how cute and funny her child was, the childless woman decides that she's ready to be a mother. She saw the cute side of motherhood, but not the price of being a mother.

Some years ago, I had a Siberian Husky

named Xavier. Xavier was my pride and joy and I loved him dearly. Xavier lived in the house with me and I spent a lot of time talking to him. I helped him to identify certain words, and this wasn't hard to do considering Siberian Huskies are a very smart breed. It wasn't long before Xavier was responding to the words I spoke to him. For example, when I told him to go upstairs, he would rush up the stairs and into the empty bedroom he considered to be his room. Anytime I asked him if he wanted to go outside, he'd rush to the front door, jump around excitedly and bark until I took him outside. When I asked him questions, he would howl and whimper as if he was trying to answer me. Many of my friends noticed how intelligent, happy and funny he was, so they decided that they wanted dogs as well. Some even wanted huskies, but they were hard to come by in Mississippi, so they settled for whatever dogs they could get. At first, I was excited because they were all going to animal shelters and getting their dogs, but my excitement was short-lived. It wasn't long before they began to complain about the responsibilities of having a dog, and it wasn't long before their dogs died from some form of neglect or they'd given them away. The point is... there are some men out there who want wives because they've seen their friends and family members in what they perceived to be happy marriages. They began to associate having wives with being happy, so they rushed off to the clubs, churches, malls or wherever women gathered, and they exchanged numbers with the women who caught their eyes. It wasn't long before they were fornicating with those women, and it wasn't long before some of the women were pregnant or some of the guys had married their new love interests. Of course, after responsibility came on the scene, those relationships changed and eventually ended. The truth was that none of them were ready for serious, long-term commitments. They simply saw something they thought they wanted based on their perceptions of it. That's why it's important to be hidden in the Lord, because believe it or not, some men who are in full submission to God are eager to get married, even though they aren't ready. Why aren't they ready? Even though they're in full submission to God, the Lord is still helping them to develop the godly character of a husband. They've given their hearts to God, but God is still working on their hearts to repair the damage done by some of the people who've influenced their lives: (mothers, fathers, ex-girlfriends, ex-wives, their own children, siblings, churches, etc.). Sure, they would make decent husbands in their current conditions, but decent isn't good enough when you're under attack. God has to teach them to be protectors of their families, to cover their wives and provide for their homes. He has to deliver them from cultural mindsets, religiousness, familiar traditions and any ungodly relationships they are currently a part of. In other words, they would be "good enough" husbands until their hearts were tried, and that's when their marriages would fall apart. God teaches them to stand so they won't fall for the Devil's devices once they take on the roles of husbands. The same goes for many single women, of course. Many of you think you're ready for marriage, but you're not. You seek the perks and benefits of marriage, but you're ignoring the reality of marriage, meaning, you don't know if you can handle the responsibilities. Knowing how to cook, clean and submit sexually to a man is not enough to sustain a marriage. You have to know how to stand in the face of adversity and not be moved by what you see, but rather move the adversary with your faith. You have to know how to separate the Devil

from your husband when the two of you
are not getting along, otherwise, you will
rebuke your husband and try to cast him
out, when it's the Devil who needs to be
rebuked and sent away. Because of this,
God has to ready the hearts of His
daughters to be the wives they've prayed to
be. While He's preparing your hearts, He
covers and hides you from God-fearing men
who are seeking their wives because it
would be easy for them to mistake another
man's wife-in-waiting for their own. This is
especially true when the wife-in-waiting has
everything they've been praying or hoping
for in their own wives.

Of course, some God-fearing men will
notice wives-in-waiting, but they won't be
able to "see" them. This means that they'll
notice a woman's characteristics, outer
beauty and some of the qualities they want
in their wives, but they won't see the
hidden desires of her heart. They won't see

who she is within, so they'll seek to get to know her as she is, but would not welcome who she's called to be once she begins to transition. This means that they would stunt a woman's spiritual growth if she were to marry them. The way to avoid such an individual is to simply pray about him, ask him pointed questions about what he wants in a wife and to simply be yourself. A man will always tell you who he is if you'll only listen with the right set of ears. If you listen with your carnal mind, you'll hear his potential, but if you listen in the realm of truth, you'll hear the truth and the truth will set you free.

Hidden in Plain Sight

One of the hardest things for a wife-in-waiting to endure is being hidden in plain sight. A lot of women complain about being noticed by the wrong types of men, but a wife hidden in plain sight often complains about not being noticed by any men. The light of God radiates through her and scares away men who are walking in darkness, but somehow, the men in her church or any church she attends never seem to notice her. The ones who do notice her are oftentimes a lot older than herself. In growing her up to be a wife, God has placed a level of maturity in her that is attractive to older men, but can be somewhat intimidating to men her own age. This can be confusing to a wife-in-waiting and it causes many to believe that they need to change churches, move to another city, or in some cases, move to another state to be found by their God-appointed husbands. It goes without saying, however, that this is not true. A wife-in-waiting simply needs to be still and know that He (JEHOVAH) is God.

Before a wife-in-waiting is hidden in plain sight, she finds herself in a season of being sifted, but not by the Devil. The Lord sometimes sifts us to help us to see within ourselves what He sees in us. He helps us to get past all of the religious jargon we speak, our understandings, our acts and our titles to see what's hiding beneath the surface of our hearts. The truth is that we can sometimes blind ourselves to the truth by choosing to see what we do for God, rather than observing what we do to God. When we get into such a dark place, the Lord will oftentimes turn on the light of truth in our lives to reveal to us the sin we've learned to turn a blind eye to.

Once a wife-in-waiting enters her season of being hidden, she will see her progress in the Lord. She will notice how differently she thinks and she will notice many of the changes God has made to her life. Many of her old friends will go away, and many of her new friends will be people she's never considered being friends with. Every friendship a woman enters represents her state of mind, and every time she exits an old mindset, the loss of friendships represent her arrival at a new place in Christ. During this season, she may question her wait more because she will recognize that she is fully submitted to God. She will recognize that she's practicing abstinence because she loves and fears the Lord; not because she's trying to manipulate Him into sending her a husband. She will recognize her heart for God and His people. At that time, she will understand that she is ready to be found by her God-appointed husband, but the fact that she hasn't been found yet may be confusing to her. She has been processed and she's no longer considered a mere woman who desires to be married, but she is now a wife who is waiting for her husband. She has been tried and tested and she has passed every test that's come her way, yet and still, her husband will not have arrived to claim her as his good thing from the Lord. Because of this, she may question whether she's sinned against God somehow, somewhere along the wait. She may question whether the wait was necessary. She may over-analyze conversations she's had and some of the things she's done. A few of the questions a wife hidden in plain sight will ask herself include, but are not limited to:

- Did my argument with _____ set me back?
- Did I delay the arrival of my husband when I _____?
- Did I somehow miss God?

- Does God really choose our mates for us?
- Was the Prophet who spoke to me about my God-appointed husband a false prophet?
- Was _____ the husband God chose for me? Maybe I rejected the wrong man!

Again, the problem is that she recognizes that she is ready to be found, but she doesn't understand why so many men pass her by. No man has stepped forward to claim her, even though she is a rare and valuable jewel.

There may be many reasons why no man has stepped forward to claim her, including the reality that *her* husband may not be ready yet. The truth is... many women prepare themselves to be found by their God-appointed husbands, but they rarely take the time to consider that their husbands may not be quite ready. This isn't a bad thing because if the wife-in-waiting arrives at a place of maturity, she can successfully begin to intercede on behalf of her husband. After all, God knows who her husband is.

Another possible reason she hasn't been claimed yet is... it may not be the season for her to meet her husband. Please understand that when God readies us to be found by our husbands, He isn't doing it for them (the husbands), He is maturing us so that we can draw closer to Himself. Once we enter our seasons of maturity, even though we are ready for marriage, we still have to wait for God to bring us together with the men He has chosen to cover, protect, lead and provide for us. This doesn't mean that a wife-in-waiting has waited for nothing; it simply means that God wants her to Himself, for Himself and by herself for a season, and that, in itself, is a blessing.

When a woman is hidden in plain sight, she won't be easily noticed by the men who are in submission to God, but she will be noticed by the Ishmaels in her church. As a reminder, God told Abraham that He was going to bless him with a son, even though Abraham was an elderly man married to an elderly woman (Sarah). Sarah doubted that she could birth any children because she was ninety years old, so she gave her handmaiden, Hagar, to Abraham to marry. Of course, back then, they didn't have official weddings, so Abraham basically married Hagar by simply sleeping with her. Hagar became pregnant and bore a son for Abraham... a son Abraham named Ishmael. Ishmael was not the promised son, but he was an act of the flesh and a manifestation of Sarah's doubt. Abraham would go on to have the promised son with his wife and he named their son Isaac. So, when you hear people in ministry referring to a man as an Ishmael, they are basically saying that he is not the man God sent for whichever woman he's romantically involved with.

One thing about an Ishmael is that he always looks like the promise. You must absolutely have an intimate relationship with God and be able to hear and discern His voice to get past an Ishmael because most Ishmaels cannot be discerned with our carnal understandings. With that being said, many of the men who approach single wives-in-waiting aren't Ishmaels because they don't look, sound or behave like the promised man. Instead, they are mere men who simply see women they're interested in. Their sin is almost always on display, which means that to be with them, we have to intentionally close our eyes and ignore the truth. Most women unknowingly court Ishmaels because they think the men pursuing them are their appointed Isaacs.

To discern an Ishmael, a woman must be in full submission to God, have her mind made up that she isn't going to settle for any man but the one God has chosen for her, and she must be led by God in her communications with the man in question. For example, when a man from my past tried to reenter my life, he came looking like the promised man. As a matter of fact, he was very similar to the man my Apostle had seen in a vision. There were a few differences, but not enough to set off any major alarms. To discern him, I had to be willing to accept that he may not be the promised man and he wasn't. A lot of women pray about men that they've already made their minds up about. My flesh wanted him to be the one, but after speaking with him, I knew he wasn't my God-appointed husband. I could've written off some of the wrong things he'd said to favor all of the right things he said, but I could not pull the wool over my own eyes again. To be with him, I would have to enter that relationship knowing full well that he wasn't the promised man. I would have to enter that relationship the same way I entered my previous marriages: believing that I could change him and focusing more on his potential than the reality of who he has chosen to be. He wanted most of the things I wanted, but he was not the man of promise and I could not get around that fact. So, I came face-to-face with a choice: Continue talking with a man whom God has not sent to me or wait for the promise. I chose to end all communications with my ex and wait for the promise. My choice represented my faith. After all, the ex was a true Ishmael and a quality one at that. He wanted many of the things I wanted, but I didn't focus as much on myself as I did on the Lord when speaking with him. I realized that having a relationship with him would not give God the glory, but instead, would put me in the same predicament I'd found myself in during the previous two marriages I'd entered. The point is we can be hidden in plain sight, but that does not mean we're invisible. It simply means that true men of God will have trouble seeing us, and the enemy will use that time to shoot Ishmaels at us. Make no mistake about it... an Ishmael is a weapon formed against a woman and her God-given assignment in life. He is weapon formed against the children she is scheduled to bear for her husband. He is a weapon against the ministry she is supposed to have with her husband. An Ishmael is a weapon formed by Satan to derail a woman or a wife-in-waiting and keep her from being found by her God-appointed husband.

When you're hidden in plain sight, you have to remember that God is faithful and everything He has spoken regarding you will come to pass. You simply need to stay in

His will and refuse to be moved. Satan will send some quality Ishmaels your way, and the closer you get to the appointed man of God, the better quality the Ishmael will be who Satan shoots at you. But if your mind is made up to serve and worship the Lord by waiting for the one He has appointed for your life, you'll get past the Ishmaels and you'll make it through the seasons where you're hidden in plain sight.

The Seasons of Loneliness

I was going through a divorce and on my
own for the first time in my life. I lived
more than eight hundred miles away from
my family, I had no children, I didn't have
any friends in Florida and the Lord hadn't
released me to attend any of the churches
near me, so I didn't have a church family. I
was truly alone, but God had prepared me
for my season of loneliness.

I'd spent the last five years married to an
adulterous man who traveled out of state
or out of the country at least once every
other month. Of course, anytime I insisted
on traveling with him, he insisted that I
could not go because his trips were either
labeled as business trips or he'd say that he
was visiting his sister. His sister and I didn't

get along. After spending a week or two alone every other month, I'd somewhat adapted to being alone. I stopped complaining about my situation and I changed my perspective on it. I no longer saw myself as a victim, but I began to see myself as a woman of God on a long, annoying, but necessary God-purposed journey to my promised land. I knew that if I would stay in submission to God and just trust Him with my life, He would bring me to a better place eventually. I knew that God had already picked out my destination and He'd already decided whether the husband I'd chosen for myself was going to accompany me to that destination or not. I simply needed to stay in faith.

In addition to being lonely, I was going through the grieving process of watching another marriage die a slow and agonizing death. Nevertheless, I reminded myself that for the entire length of my marriage to my ex, I had been lonely, even though the two of us were living under the same roof, sleeping in the same bed and riding in the same car. A lot of women don't realize that loneliness doesn't end when you're married; it ends when you've become content with yourself. I was married and more lonely than I'd ever been. After my ex and I finally separated, I found myself alone for the first time in my life, but I can't say that I was more lonely than I was when I was with him.

What I found about loneliness is that it's not only a choice, but it reveals the condition of our hearts. First and foremost, I chose to forgive my ex, and then, I chose to make the best of my season of singleness. I knew that the choice was mine. I could choose to be a victim, and as a victim, I could cry, complain and become bitter about the predicament I'd found myself in or I could see my situation from a different set of eyes

and choose to make the best of it. I chose
the latter. Through forgiveness, I didn't
blame my ex for my loneliness. Instead, I
blamed myself. If I'd obeyed God and
stayed in His will, I wouldn't have found
myself married to another man whom God
had not given permission to have me,
which, in turn, translated to me not having
to go through another divorce. I began to
see my ex as the victim, but at the same
time, I did not beat myself up for my
mistake. I decided to be happy. I decided
to trust God. I decided to move on with my
life. I decided to remain abstinent and walk
in the spirit of holiness. I decided to follow
God all the way, and because of the
decisions I made, God decided to protect,
provide for and keep me.

Loneliness is a choice, but being alone isn't
always a choice. After having to be
delivered from so many ungodly friendships
and associations, I came to understand that

God will repeatedly, and sometimes, loudly remove the people from our lives who we've brought with us on our life's journeys. Bringing people into our lives who He has to evict will oftentimes delay the very things we've been praying for because we have to be delivered from the soul ties, mindsets and the residue brought on by those friendships and associations. Some of the things that were set in motion by the words released in those relationships have to be stopped. To make matters worse, this often restarts our seasons of being alone and delays the very thing we've been praying for.

I chose not to be lonely, even though I was alone. I did this by choosing to busy myself with my God-given purpose, rather than complaining about where I was and how I'd gotten there. There were times when I felt lonely, but I knew that I could do something about my loneliness. I didn't have to sit in my apartment and submit to my situation. Just like most of you, I had options. I joined a gym, did a lot of walking, took myself out to eat often and went wherever I wanted to go. When I decided that I wanted to have a friend who lived near me to hang out with sometimes, I prayed about it and God arranged a meeting between me and a woman who would prove to be a very dear friend.

I was about to go for my daily walk one day when I spotted a woman I'd seen walking a few times. We were on opposite sides of the road, and I was preparing to cross the street when I saw her. I was putting my earbud in my ear and preparing to listen to another Creflo Dollar sermon when she spotted me. She gestured for me to come and walk with her, and from that day forward, we became good friends. Like me, she was divorced, lived alone and didn't have any children. She lived in the

condominiums next to my apartment
building, just a minute's walk away from
me. We agreed to walk together everyday
and the occasional loneliness issue was
resolved. I suddenly had a friend who was
similar to me in many ways and she turned
out to be a huge blessing in my life.

The point is... loneliness doesn't have to be
resolved by entering ungodly friendships,
unequally yoked relationships or reconciling
with unpleasant family members.
Loneliness is not the condition of being
alone, since some people are content with
being alone. Loneliness is how you respond
to being alone. In addition, as I mentioned
earlier, a person can be married and still be
lonely, just as I was. Some women respond
to being alone by surrounding themselves
with people but that's not always the best
solution. Oftentimes, it delays their arrivals
at the places and situations they've been
praying to be in. Just as people have to be

delivered from demons, we often have to
be delivered from demon-possessed or
demonically influenced people. That's why
it is better to let God form your friendships,
and anytime He doesn't send anyone into
your life, it is better to spend that season
seeking His face all the more.

One of the blessings that being alone offers
us is the ability to be better wives to our
God-appointed husbands when they arrive.
How so? It keeps us from being too clingy
and too needy. It also helps us to not
become hindrances to our husbands by
complaining anytime they have to go
somewhere without us. For example, let's
say your husband is in ministry and even
though the two of you always travel
together, you've just discovered that you're
pregnant and the doctor has advised
against you traveling. However, your
husband has a ministry engagement
coming up and he's going to be out of town

for the next few days. How would you respond? The average woman would feel threatened and unsure because being without her husband is something she's not used to. It takes her outside of her comfort zone, and because of this, she would become argumentative. Nevertheless, a woman who has discovered her own self worth and has been through the seasons of loneliness, won't see her husband's impending absence as a dreadful event; she would see it as a hiccup in their lives. Sure, it's not what she wants, but she knows that he'll be back home in a few days. Some women will even embrace his absence and utilize it to do some of the things they couldn't ordinarily do when he's at home like spring (or winter) cleaning, rearranging furniture, spending the day at the spa and the list goes on. If you can't handle being alone while you're alone, you won't make a good wife unless your husband is without purpose and just as clingy as you are.

Don't throw away or complain about your alone time. Instead, spend that time with the Lord. Below are 12 tips to help you during your seasons of loneliness.

1. Understand that you're alone, but you don't have to be lonely. Loneliness is a mindset and not a state of existing. If you change your mind about being alone, you'll change your attitude. I often told myself that I was on a flight headed to the place I'd been praying for, but if I wanted to get there, I had to stay on the plane. I understood that each day represented me being another day closer to what I'd been praying for, but more than that, I decided to not focus on where I was heading. I decided to focus on the day that I was living in and to make the best of it.

2. Get busy in your purpose. An idle woman is a pest to herself and

anyone who embraces her. What's amazing is that I've met a lot of women who were not operating in their God-given purposes and they became annoyances to me... and I was just a friend! They called too much and wanted to talk about everything that they'd witnessed, from the smallest events to the greatest. At first, I would entertain their boredom until I realized that it was costing me to entertain them. After a while, I had to start avoiding many of their calls. If they were a nuisance to me, I can only imagine how much of a nuisance they'd be to their husbands. Get busy! There is purpose on the inside of you; get in it and learn to be who you are gifted to be. A woman who's busy being who she is won't end up being a busy body!

3. Seek the kingdom of God with all

your might. Now, this one has to be
number one on your list! The Bible
tells us to seek first the kingdom of
God and all His righteousness and
everything else will be added to us. I
can't stress to you how important it is
to seek the face of God with all your
heart, strength and might first and
foremost. This will help you to get
past you and overcome the enemy
that uses you against yourself. This
will help you to know God more so
that you will love Him more and
offend Him less. This will help you to
get to know yourself more, thus,
making it easier for you to turn down
the wrong man, because you'll have
faith that the right one is on his way.

4. Learn something new everyday. One
of the things I've learned is that the
human brain is the belly of our souls
and knowledge is the meat it needs
to survive. Without knowledge, the

soul will perish and the person bearing the soul will esteem or reverence the wrong people. For example, a woman with little to no knowledge will look up to a foolish woman she thinks is smarter than herself. When you meet your husband, you want to have something to talk about besides your past or present conditions. You need knowledge to be a wife and you need knowledge to be the help meet you are designed to be. For me, I often learn a new word, a new bit of history, a new skill or I acquire more knowledge about the kingdom of God every day that I live. This helps me to keep my mind sharp and to find new interests to embrace. After all, I don't want to be a woman limited by the lack of knowledge. Instead, I want to continue to embrace new opportunities. You can even learn a new language, learn to cook different dishes or learn to swim. The choice is yours.

5. Limit your idle time and spend more time being productive. The more time you spend being idle, and that includes being on the phone with other idle people, the more time you'll spend in the season you're in. Seasons aren't designed to stick around; they are designed to help you to birth out of you whatever God has planted in you. Each season readies you for the next season of your life. If you spend time being idle, you'll reap an idle man's reward: nothing but more time to be idle with and more idle people to waste your time on. For example, you should limit your phone conversations to thirty minutes to an hour every other day. Remember, you cannot reap what you have not sown, but if you

spend too much time doing nothing, you're going to spend a lot of time reaping nothing.

6. Get involved in your community more. Get out and feed the homeless, clean up your neighborhood or volunteer at an orphanage. The possibilities are endless because there are a lot of people who could use your help.

7. If you have the love, time, funds and the patience, get yourself a pet. When I was going through my divorce and I felt stable enough to get a pet, I went to my local shelter and got myself a dog. I prayed about that decision for three months because I wanted to make sure that I had the patience and the funds to give him the home he deserved. I didn't want to be a self-centered pet owner, only getting a dog to entertain me. Instead, I wanted to rescue a dog and

be a blessing to him. A lot of people get pets, and then, return them to the shelters simply because they wanted the perks of pet ownership without the responsibilities of being pet owners. This increases the risk of a dog or cat being euthanized because pets are less desirable for adoption as they age. They have a greater chance at being adopted into a forever-home when they are younger than they do when they're two years of age or older. That's why it's never a great idea to "try on" pet ownership; instead, whenever you decide to get a pet, make sure you're in it for the long haul.

8. Study yourself and get to know you more. I paid attention to my habits and my downfalls. I prayed about any stronghold I found myself bound by and I intentionally set out to create good habits. For example, I

noticed that I would use up the paper towels or tissue that was on a roll and I would not replace it until I needed it again. That was a bad habit, so I sought to end that habit, and nowadays, I have a habit of replacing the rolls whenever they're empty. I also had a bad habit of buying things when I needed them, but nowadays, I habitually buy all of my necessities in bulk. I don't wait until I'm down to my last roll of paper towels to go to the store. Once I have a single pack of paper towels left, I'll buy another pack or two whenever I go to the store. This new habit will undoubtedly help me to be a better help meet to my husband. Pay attention to yourself and ask yourself what habits need to be done away with and what new habits you want to acquire. Creating new habits and ending old habits have to be done intentionally.

9. Do for yourself what you want a man to do for you. Ask yourself this question: What is it that you want your husband to do for you that you've never thought about doing for yourself? Did you know that the average woman associates certain events and extracurricular activities with men? For example, the Lord told me to go out to eat by myself, so when I was in Florida, I'd dress up every Saturday and go out to one of my favorite restaurants. When I tell this to women, a lot of them say that I'm courageous because they couldn't fathom the idea of eating out alone. That's because they've been taught that dining out is for couples only. At first, dining out alone felt different to me, but the Lord started teaching me to dine by myself when I was still married. After a while, it felt great

(and empowering) to sit in a restaurant and order whatever I wanted while sitting by myself. I didn't feel awkward because I didn't care or think about what others thought of me. Many of the waitresses in my favorite restaurants came to know my face, and they'd seat me at the booth they knew I preferred. I didn't look at the women who were out with their guys and feel sorry for myself. Instead, I felt sorry for many of the women I saw dining out. It felt good to know that I could easily go and get a guy if I wanted to, but I'd chosen to be alone and wait on the God-appointed husband. I loved dressing up and letting the Lord take me out to eat. There are many things you can do; for example, start traveling to other cities and states; if you have the time and the funds to travel abroad, do so.

The more you do for yourself and by yourself, the more content you'll become in your singleness. The woman I met while walking in Florida had her own condominium, a new car, a great job and she had her own money. She wasn't rich, but she lived comfortably and she traveled a lot. She didn't sit around and complain about being alone; she did something about it. Because of this, she wasn't anxious to have a man. The more she did for herself or allowed God to do for her, the higher she set the bar for the man who would one day have the pleasure and the blessing of calling her his wife.

10. Don't feed your soul junk food media such as secular music and reality television. The truth is... music encourages us, discourages us, influences us and has the power to tell us how to feel. One nice slow jam

on a rainy day could make you feel so
sorry for yourself that you'd pick up
the phone and call whichever ex the
song reminded you of. There is
power in music and there is power in
what you watch. Watch shows that
empower you to be a better person.
For example, I watch a lot of shows
about buying, selling and refacing
properties. If nothing else, I used
those shows to learn more about real
estate, both domestic and abroad, so
they often ended up helping me
complete number four on this list:
Learn something new everyday.

11. Make sure your bills are manageable.
    If you don't watch a lot of television,
    you probably don't need cable. Home
    phones are pretty much a thing of the
    past and you can now get affordable
    cell phone service without the
    bondage of a contractual agreement.
    I cut off my cable and got Netflix, I

ordered a MagicJack for phone service (even though I didn't need it truthfully) and I lived by a rule that I learned from my ex-husband: If you can't afford to pay for it with cash, don't mess with it. My monthly bills consisted of nothing but my rent and my utilities. I purchased a car for $3,600 and paid the insurance up for six months at a time. A lot of people would say that they can't afford to do this, but that's not always true. Getting my car was a faith move for me, especially since I was alone for the first time in my life and I hadn't saved up a lot of money. I was used to my ex-husband paying most of the bills. Nevertheless, I found that most people get a lump sum of money every year during tax season and some people get checks back from school. The problem is that they spend that money on vain things, scattering all of it around their cities. I watched a friend of mine, who, by the way, was on public assistance, use her income tax check to pay up her rent for six months, pay off her car note for six months and pay for her car insurance for six months every time she got her taxes. After that, she lived great throughout the year, and whenever she got her school check back, she would pay off her rent, car note and car insurance for another six months. I decided to do the same, even though I didn't have the added luxury of public assistance. I bought my car with cash (no car notes), paid off my insurance for six months and created what I referred to as a rent account. With my rent account, I had checkbooks that I only used to pay my rent. I didn't touch that account for any other reason except to pay my rent. I didn't even monitor the money in that account except to occasionally make sure that nothing had been stolen. Know this: a woman who is in financial bondage will easily give herself to the wrong man for the right price. I don't mean that she would prostitute herself, but I do mean that if a man who appears to be decent came along, and he made what she thought was "good money", it is very likely that she would enter a relationship and possibly a marriage with him because life with him appears easier.

12. Find women on social media and locally (if God permits) who've successfully waited for their God-appointed husbands... women who have traveled the path you're on. Don't spend too much time with women who are still on that journey because if they fail, they'd make it

harder for you to stand. Instead, encourage women who are on the path you're on, but follow women who've made it to where you're headed. You'll notice that this journey is not for the faint at heart, and one-by-one, many women fall for the devices of the enemy while taking this faith-walk. They leave this path of righteousness and holiness to follow the men Satan sent to distract, derail and destroy them. If you link yourself with such women, you will be extremely discouraged when the one you thought was the greatest or strongest among them falls. Nevertheless, if you follow women who've successfully followed God, you will come to the end of yourself and see how important and easy it is to do the same if you simply make up your mind to do so. For some women, waiting on the appointed

husband is a religious garment
they're trying on, hoping that their
abstinence and their words will
produce the husbands they want to
erect as idols in their lives. Not
understanding that God truly sees
and knows their uncommitted hearts,
they honestly think they've convinced
Him that He is number one in their
lives. After waiting year after year (or
sometimes a few months), many of
these women turn their backs on God
and find their own men to idolize.
The wait is only successful if it is used
as a tool of worship to God; it
cannot be a tool to get what you
want. If abstinence is only done to
get a husband, it is not abstinence; it
is an attempt to manipulate God.
Instead, the woman using this tool of
manipulation is simply a fornicator
who's refraining from having sex in
hopes that her closed legs will

convince God to send her a husband. God said that if we love Him, we are to keep His commandments. For God, it's all about love because He is love, so build your relationship with Him and don't focus so much on being some man's wife if you have not learned to be a faithful daughter to God.

The seasons of loneliness are a small price to pay for what God has in store for you.

1 Corinthians 2:9: But, as it is written, "What no eye has seen, nor ear heard, nor the heart of man imagined, what God has prepared for those who love him."

I am absolutely convinced that God has better taste than I do, and I know that what He has planned for me greatly supersedes what I have planned for myself. I had to give up on me and start trusting in Him and so should you. In my seasons of being alone, I've chosen not to be lonely, but to stay busy. I have learned more about God and myself in this season, and this new knowledge has helped to keep me from entering relationships with the wrong men. The enemy upped his ante and started sending what some would refer to as "quality Ishmaels" my way, but I rejected them all in favor of the one whose rib I am. I chose to remain alone until my other half finds me, instead of being lonely and settling for a counterfeit.

Pride Versus Progress

I've been married and divorced twice because I married when I was but a babe in Christ. I was God's rebellious child who went into sin, came out with sinners, and then, tried to drag their resistant bodies to church with me. I thought they just needed to hear the truth and have those devils cast out of them, and then, they'd make great husbands. After being physically and verbally abused and repeatedly cheated on, I came to a new understanding: I didn't make a great match-maker for myself and I could not change a man. I also came to realize that doing the right things for the wrong man is like trying to breast-feed a rattlesnake and hoping for the best. I didn't know who I was in Christ; Satan knew more about my calling than I did. He knew that I

would someday minister to single and
married couples alike and that's why he
attacked me in the area of relationships. He
wanted to discredit me, but instead, the
Lord used those broken marriages to teach
me how to overcome adversity and be a
better wife.

Nowadays, I counsel married couples and
I've found that the most common spirit that
comes against marriages is the spirit of
pride, or better yet, the spirit of self-
righteousness. Basically, people bound by
this spirit have unknowingly erected
themselves as idols. They don't operate as
one person with their spouses; instead,
they make marriage all about themselves.
They take it upon themselves to determine
the temperature of their marriages based
on what their spouses do or have not done
for them. For example, a self-centered man
plans to watch football for an entire day.
His wife is not a football lover, so she

decides to spend the day at a friend's house. The self-righteous husband gets offended because he wanted his wife to be home with him, even though he knows that if she stays home, she would most likely be in a different room watching something else on television. After the wife insists on spending the day with her friend, the husband decides to teach her a lesson. Instead of watching the football game at home, he leaves and spends the day at the house of one of his old, and not-so-decent friends, David. Initially, he told his wife that he was no longer going to deal with David because he was a thieving, cheating low-life with a foul mouth. But to teach his wife a lesson, he spends the day at David's house and he's sure to come home late so that his wife will notice his absence. When he returns home, he boasts to his wife that he spent the day with David. When she questions his choice, he utilizes that opportunity to vent about her choice to spend the day with her friend instead of him. After that, the husband stops speaking to the wife for a few days, because in his mind, the lesson needs to stick so that she understands that her happiness is tied to his happiness. That's a self-righteous and prideful spirit in full operation. The husband couldn't see past himself, and because of this, he took it upon himself to act as his wife's judge and jury. He sentences her to days or weeks of getting the cold-shoulder because he wants to ensure that she never puts her happiness above his contentment. The couple remains married for three years before divorcing because the wife slowly loses respect for her husband and there isn't enough room in their house for the husband's monstrous pride and his wife. Believe it or not, this is a common story in marriage. Many marriages die because one or both parties in them can't see past their own happiness. It is not uncommon for

married people to see themselves as victims
and start sowing days, months and years of
discord into their marriages, hoping to reap
the marriages they want. Of course, this
doesn't happen and the marriages are
slowly put to death because selfishness is
toxic to marriages. That's why it is
absolutely important to be delivered from
pride and self-righteousness while you're
single, otherwise, your marriage would be
doomed from the moment you said, "I do."

After the Lord showed me the strongman of
pride that's behind the majority of failed
marriages, He helped me to better
understand why He wants us to seek the
Kingdom of God first before we seek to be
some man's wife. The truth is that we are
selfish by nature, but the Word of God
delivers us from this sinful selfishness and
helps us to see the bigger picture. We
begin to see life outside of our own
reflections and God teaches us to love our

brethren as we love ourselves. This process is the act of dying to one's self and being willing to invest your time and money to help your fellow man. What's happening is... God is giving us His heart and teaching us to see the world from Heaven's eyes. This form of deliverance not only helps us to grow closer to God and win more souls for the kingdom of God, but it also helps us to be better wives to the men God has appointed to lead us. It even helps us to attract the husbands who God has chosen for our lives.

When we seek the kingdom of God, we begin to wear a sweet mist that could best be described as the perfume of holiness. This sweet smell attracts our husbands, but only after they are also clothed in holiness and faithfully seeking the face and favor of God. This means that we all come outside of ourselves, thus, disengaging the strongmen (pride) who likes to use our flesh against us. We become more selfless and less selfish. Like attracts like, so one of God's reasons for making us more like Himself is to cause us to attract husbands who are more like Him. By doing so, we enter holy matrimony with our spouses, instead of just plain matrimony. We also birth children after God's own heart and we become a light to those who've never seen marriage done God's way.

Self-righteousness and pride must be overcome before we enter the holy union of marriage, otherwise, our selfishness will overcome our marriages and evict us from them. That's because it is very difficult for a prideful person to see the error of their own ways, and this causes them to magnify the flaws of any and everyone around them. Self-righteous people blame their wrong choices on the choices and words of others. They often credit themselves when things are going their way, but they see themselves as victims when things are not turning in their favor. Because of this, when prideful people are offended, they often feel the need to get revenge against the person or people who've offended them. This includes their spouses and their very own children. This is to get you to understand why it's absolutely necessary for you to be delivered from self-righteous thinking so that you can be a God-sent wife who's married to her God-sent husband.

Self-righteousness and pride are divisive spirits that discourage unity and promote division by causing one or both spouses to become spiritually nearsighted. In other words, a nearsighted saint can't see too far outside of himself or herself. Believe it or not, the majority of people who are available for marriage are shortsighted and that's why many people are overly anxious to get married. They see marriage as a way to fix their own issues, and when self-

seeking people get married in this state of
mind, they often spend countless days and
nights trying to "tame" their spouses.

Again, in counseling couples, I have found
that this is one of the most common devices
of a self-centered person. They end up
having bipolar marriages, whereas, they will
reward their spouses when they do what
they want, but they will often punish
(sometimes severely) their spouses for
disappointing them. Of course, some are
worse than others, but either way, the
marriage ends up becoming an institution
of bondage rather than an institution of
love.

How do you overcome self-righteousness
and pride? First and foremost, please know
that God will not send your man of God to
you when you're prideful and self-seeking
(in most cases). In the rare cases that He
allows a self-centered man to find his self-
centered wife, it's because He has a plan for

that couple. They would likely go on to
fight as prideful people do, and then,
separate and sometimes divorce one
another until they finally come together
God's way. They would then be used by
God to minister to other couples about
overcoming adversity in marriage. Now,
this sounds like a great ministry to have
with your spouse, which I'm sure it is, but
understand that a couple like that will take
one another through a lot of headaches and
heartaches because of their pride. This
means that they've had to overcome a lot.
They've had to overcome offenses that the
average couple would not know how to
overcome. They've hurt one another
beyond human comprehension. They've
had to die to themselves while married and
this is no easy task to do because dying to
self is not an attractive process. They've
had to repeatedly forgive one another for
their crimes against each other and they've
had to go back to the starting line of their

marriages time and time again until they got past themselves, got over their offenses and fully submitted themselves to God. In layman's terms, you don't want their testimony! It is better to die to yourself while single than it is to go through that process while married.

Below are five tips to overcoming pride and self-righteousness.

1. Acknowledge that you have a problem. Pay attention to yourself and how you treat others. How many times in a day do you complain about something someone has done to or has not done for you? A person who complains a lot is oftentimes a self-centered person. If you notice that you are selfish, you need to admit it to yourself and God. That's the only way you'll seek to get past yourself to embrace a love that goes beyond your understanding.

2. Seek the kingdom of God like never before. This one often seems to be the hardest of them all, but in all truth, it's the easiest thing to do. The problem is that the flesh wants to stay in control, so the flesh will rebel against anything that threatens its position. Notwithstanding, you have to seek the face of God and seek to please the Lord with all of your heart, mind and soul so that He can bring you into a knowledge of yourself that will help you to get over yourself.

3. Get out and help others. First and foremost, when you decide to become selfless and help others, you will notice how great of a fight your flesh will put up against you. Nevertheless, get out and help those who are less fortunate than yourself. This will help you to empathize more with others and understand their struggles.

4. Practice with the people in your own house. Spend time doing kind things for the people in your household without expecting anything in return. As a matter of fact, when you do something kind for someone, you should never remind them of what you've done for them. If you do boast about your works, your motivation for doing it was completely selfish, meaning, you have not moved forward. You've simply found another way to manipulate a situation to make it point back to you. Get over yourself so that God can send you the husband you've been praying for.

5. Ask God to help you with your journey. Getting past your flesh and getting over yourself is a journey in itself. As a matter of fact, it is one of the hardest journeys you will ever put your feet to and it is something you

can't do alone. You need God to guide you, lift you up and strengthen you as you journey closer to the heart of God.

Praying for the Husband You Haven't Met

During my season of singleness, the Lord taught me to pray for my God-appointed husband. I had to start interceding on his behalf, even though I didn't know his name, what he looked like or when I would meet him. This wasn't just an act of obedience, it was an act of faith and it helped me to realize that I was not praying for "a" man, but I was praying for "the" man God had already appointed for me. There wasn't a pool of men who were being tested to see who would be a better fit for me. There was (and is) one specific man who's already passed the test, and the test had little or nothing to do with me. It had everything to do with his relationship with God.

Interceding on my husband's behalf didn't put a face on him, but it did make him more real to me. The more real he became to me, the more determined I was not to entertain any other man. It wasn't long before I realized that God was teaching me to love a man I hadn't yet met. He was teaching me to respect my husband, even though I hadn't met him. After all, experience has taught me a very valuable lesson, and that is... husbands do care about the past behaviors of their wives. I learned this lesson when I was married the first time.

I was married to my first husband and I was freshly saved. I was the very definition of a babe in Christ, so I still thought and reasoned like the world. It goes without saying that I was married to a worldly man because we always attract what we are. I lived in Greenville, Mississippi... a city where the population is a little over 40,000 residents, and even though that's not a small number, most people in Greenville know one another or know of one another. My then husband had heard about some of my past behaviors, and he was putting pressure on me to give him every detail of my past sexual exploits, but I refused. I was ashamed of my past; after all, I was still a babe in Christ and I didn't want to change his views of me. In Mississippi, the men are more conservative, so most of the women there keep their pasts a secret. One of the most popular adages that the people from Greenville live by is: *What you don't know won't hurt you.*

I lived by that adage and it became the law of my life. Nevertheless, my ex found a witness to my past who he thought was credible. That witness turned out to be one of my siblings, and even though he spoke a few truths about me, he seasoned those truths with many lies. The stories he told were far worse than the truth, so I had to slowly, but cautiously, tell my then husband about the Tiffany I once was. By remaining silent, I was allowing a picture of me to be painted in my ex's mind that did not depict the real me.

I remember being angry about my ex's almost obsessive curiosity about my past because I knew that I wasn't the same person anymore. I'd changed and I wanted him to see and love me as I was, but he was infatuated with who I once was. I say that to say this: He inquired about my sinful past because I wasn't too far removed from it. I was ashamed of my past because I hadn't been too long removed from it. Even though the old Tiffany was dead and buried, the new Tiffany didn't have a lot of history to talk about. The point is... when your husband finds you, he will want to know what you were doing while you were waiting for him. Of course, a man who's in full submission to God won't be so infatuated with who you were when you were not saved, but he will want to know how you carried yourself as a woman of God. The reason for this is... even though you may have been a young saint when you spoke, thought and behaved in an ungodly way, knowing your most recent past will help him to better understand what you've struggled with in the past. One problem you don't want is to have been a woman so obsessed with marriage that you dated a lot of men inside and outside of your church. To a man, such behavior spells desperation and no man wants to take home a woman he feels any man could have had. You need to spend your single season in the face of God and not in the faces of different men. I've seen women who erected themselves as leaders of the single-in-waiting movement fall into just about every snare thrown at them by the enemy. The enemy was making a mockery of them and showing everyone who was familiar with their ministries (or self-initiated movements) that even though they preached about waiting, they themselves could not wait.

First and foremost, to pray for the husband you haven't yet met, you must first believe that God has already chosen him. This can be very difficult if you are relying on the words of other people. For example, there are ministers out there who promote the doctrine that God does not choose our spouses for us. Most of these ministers have not consulted with God; they simply took what made sense to them and preached about it. If you haven't prayed and asked the Lord whether He's chosen your spouse or not, you will be dependent on the words of others. Basically, your faith will lean in the direction where the best sermon is preached. The whole truth is... God does choose our spouses for us if we let Him. He would prefer that we walk by faith and let Him connect us with the people He's assigned to us than for us to go out and choose our own mates. Nevertheless, a woman who chooses her own mate is not in sin if:

- He's saved.
- He's single (in the carnal and in the realm of the spirit).
- She's saved.
- She's single (in the carnal and in the realm of the spirit).
- Both parties practice a holy lifestyle and avoid fornication.
- The couple marries (in the Lord) before they have sex.

Such a couple has not sinned by courting and marrying one another, but the problem that will almost always arise is that the individuals involved in the relationship will continue to mature in Christ and learn their personal identities and assignments in the Lord. This is a good thing, but understand that anytime we marry the people we've chosen, we marry them according to where we are in Christ and how well they fit into our lives in that season of our lives. We will outgrow many of the mentalities that we pick up along our journeys, which means that the spouses we've chosen today may not fit us tomorrow. God, on the other hand, knows who we are and He knows who we're designed to be. The one He has chosen for us requires that we have faith in Him, endure and embrace our single season and that we wait for the Lord to release him in due season. The one God has chosen doesn't necessarily fit us today (especially if we haven't met him yet), but he will fit who we are as we grow up in the Lord. We're designed to grow with him and we're designed to grow because of him.

Next, we must understand who we are in Christ Jesus. If you don't yet know your purpose, you simply need to ask the Lord to reveal it to you. If you don't know who you are, you aren't ready for marriage. The reason is... you'll only introduce your husband or your future husband to the person that you think you are. As you find yourself in the Lord, you will have to continually reintroduce yourself to him and He may not like the new woman that you've become.

To know who you are, you must have an intimate relationship with Christ Jesus, and as you grow in the Lord, you'll notice that your relationship with Christ becomes less and less about you and more about Him. As you grow in the Lord, He will begin to reveal your identity to you. As you get to know you more, you'll grow to love the Lord more. That's why it's important to let God reveal the man He's assigned to your life. There will come a time that your love for God will be so great that you'll want a husband you can intimately serve and worship the Lord with. You'll become less and less selfish, and as you do, your priorities will change. Many marriages are challenged and overwhelmed because one of the people in those marriages had a change of heart. Their priorities changed and the other spouse didn't know how to adapt to the new changes around the house. For example, many marriages end when children are born because the wife will oftentimes transition from being a doting wife to a doting mother. Her husband may begin to feel left out, ignored and unimportant, and because of this, he will begin to mentally exit the marriage before he physically abandons it. Sure, this is selfish and immature, but it happens more than you know. Such a husband didn't marry his wife because he loved her; he married her because she loved and doted on him, but when a child was born to their union, he realized that he had nothing in common with his wife. Again, this is why it's important to let God choose our mates.

When you begin to understand who you are called or designed to be, you will better understand why many of the relationships you've been in did not work. This will also help you to avoid the wrong men... even the types of men you once were infatuated with.

Lastly, to successfully pray for the husband you haven't met, you must understand that marriage isn't about you. This alone changes your prayer language. Marriage is all about the kingdom of God. It is a united front designed to mirror our relationships with God, and as such, it is not a union for self-centered people. Self-centered people get married and fight their spouses, their spouses' purposes, and their own reflections because they can't see outside of what they want. Additionally, you need to wait for the one God has chosen,

otherwise, you may end up married to a
man who is self-seeking, self-centered and
selfishly motivated. Such a character is a
nightmare to be married to because he will
make every day of your marriage about
himself. Your happiness would depend on
whether he's happy. He would
unknowingly erect himself as an idol and
expect you to worship him. When you
don't exalt him above everything else, he
will judge, convict and punish you according
to the crime he feels you've committed
against him or how it made him feel. Again,
I counsel many couples and this behavior is
as common as a cold. Of course, such a
man doesn't realize he's competing with
God, but the amazing part is, when this is
brought to his attention, the average man
doesn't stop idolizing himself. He simply
apologizes to God for his behavior,
attempts to make amends with God, and
slowly, but surely, returns to his vomit
because it's hard for him to give up his god-

complex. He wants to be worshipped; he likes to be worshipped and any wife who doesn't worship him will be in danger of becoming his ex-wife or, in many cases, the victim of domestic abuse. Some women are even killed by the hands of the husbands they've chosen for themselves. God will never introduce you to a man who will someday take your life!

To start praying for your husband, you need to first make sure that God is number one in your life. Never place God in any other position in your heart and life other than the number one spot. He will never ride in the passenger's seat or the backseat of your heart! If He's number two (or any other number besides number one) in your life, and yet, you pray to Him to send the very thing you are idolizing (a husband), you are out of order with Him. Such prayers will be prayers gone amiss.

James 4:3 (KJV version): Ye ask, and receive not, because ye ask amiss, that ye may consume it upon your lusts.

James 4:3 (NIV version): When you ask, you do not receive, because you ask with wrong motives, that you may spend what you get on your pleasures.

This means that you must seek the kingdom of God before you seek to become some man's wife. Seeking the kingdom of God will cause you to slowly die to yourself so that you may live for God. In other words, this process will begin to root selfishness out of your life, and again, selfishness is the number one killer of marriage. Don't look at how selfless you feel you've been to others, because you didn't omit yourself when you were doing those things. Most people who help others (when their help is not God-motivated) are co-dependent. Some simply love the feeling of helping

others, while some love the praise and
worship of men. Some people simply love
feeling needed and wanted, while some
people help others simply because they
want to be loved and appreciated by the
people they're helping. This means that
they've earned their rewards every time
they helped others and got what they
wanted in return. You see, such behavior is
still self-centered, and when people like this
get married, they are often self-righteous
and unrepentant. They see what they've
done for others, including their spouses, but
they refuse to see their own motives; this
opens the door for the self-righteous spirit.
For example, let's create two married
characters: Michael and Susan. Michael
goes out and buys Susan a new dress, new
shoes and a new purse. He arranges for her
to get her hair done early one Saturday
morning, but by Saturday night, Michael is
furious with his wife. He has purchased
tickets for the couple to go to the theater,

and then, after the theater, he wants to take his wife out to eat, but Susan has other plans. She's about to go to her sister's birthday party... a party that Michael knew about months in advance. He knew that Susan had been invited to her sister's party, just as he'd been invited to the party, but he's not too fond of Jasmine, Susan's sister. You see, someone who hears half of this story would side with Michael, thinking his wife is an ungrateful and self-centered woman who doesn't appreciate the good man she has. But to hear the entire story, you'd understand that Michael is a manipulative, self-centered man whose good deeds are evil-centered. Michael sees the good he's done, but he refuses to look at his own selfish motives, so Susan's refusal to cancel her plans is escalated (in Michael's mind) to an offense against the marriage. For such an offense, Michael decides that Susan ought to suffer the greatest punishment for what he sees as her act of treason: Michael decides to move out of the home he shares with his wife while Susan is at her sister's birthday party. He decides to file for divorce and petition to get custody of the children he shares with his wife. Again, such behavior is VERY common and that's why it's important that you seek the kingdom of God before you even entertain the idea of being married. When you're self-centered, you will attract self-centered, self-righteous men who think life and marriage are all about themselves. I like to refer to such men as "weather-men" because they control the weather of their marriages, and they choose whether they're going to give their wives good days or rainy days based on their wives' choices to do or not do what they want.

If you've been seeking the face of God with your whole heart and you have an intimate relationship with Him, you are ready to begin praying for your husband. Below are ten things that you should pray for.

1. Pray for your husband's protection.
   Understand that the enemy wants to
   kill him and ruin God's plans for him.
2. Pray for your husband's mind. The
   mind is the battlefield; it is where
   Satan wages his wars. Send peace of
   mind and joy of heart to your
   husband. Remember, you may not
   know who the man is, but God does.
3. Pray for your husband's peace.
   Interceding for his mind is one part of
   the battle, but you also need to pray
   for his peace. A man can be in a time
   of rest, but be unable to rest because
   of the wars that have been waged
   against him in the past. Speak peace
   over your husband and ask the Lord
   to send peace to your husband
   wheresoever he is.
4. Pray for your husband's ministry.
   Understand that a saved man's life is
   his ministry, and a man without a

ministry will not be released to find his own wife. A wife is a help meet, and therefore, any man who seeks his wife must first know what he needs help with.

5. Pray for your husband's deliverance. You don't know what that man is struggling with. Understand that the word struggle means that he's in a fight for his life, purpose and sanity. Jump in the fight! Intercede on his behalf.

6. Pray against every demonic spirit, power and principality assigned to destroy, derail, intimidate or recruit your husband. Whatever you bind on earth is bound in heaven, and whatever you loose on earth is loosed in heaven.

7. Pray for your husband's career and his purpose. A man's ministry is part of his purpose, but a man's career isn't always tied to his ministry. Jesus

was a carpenter, Peter was a
fisherman, Paul was a tentmaker,
Matthew was a publican (tax
collector) and Luke was a physician
(doctor). Of course, God can and
does use what we do professionally
to minister to us and others, but
please understand that a man's
career isn't always tied to his
ministry, and that's why you need to
pray for your husband's career.

8. Pray over your husband's finances.
The enemy of God is always looking
for ways to keep God's people from
flourishing; this includes launching
attacks against our finances. A man
who cannot provide for a family
won't be released to start a family.
Cover your husband's finances with
prayer and cancel every attack
against his career and finances in the
name of Jesus.

9. Pray against every seductress,

temptress, adulteress, Jezebel, Delilah, Athaliah and ungodly woman who is assigned by Satan to derail your husband. You have the power to bind and loose. Send away from him every witch and representative of the enemy.

10. Pray for your husband's love. Understand that what's under attack is our ability to love others. Many of the attacks we've endured over the courses of our lives were attacks against our ability to love others. Many men get married while bruised, and a bruised soul will always see himself as a victim. He will repeatedly lick his wounds, and he will snarl at any person he feels is close enough to his wounded heart to further hurt him. The one person who has the power to hurt him the most is his wife, and because of this, many men who have been wounded

(when not delivered) are horrible husbands. Ask the Lord to restore your husband's love and his ability to love, but to also give him more wisdom and more discernment so he won't waste his love on the wrong people.

Praying for your husband is a wise move and it's the evidence that you are truly a wife-in-waiting if you are praying for him while in full submission to God. Make your husband a part of your daily prayer life. This will help you to better understand that you aren't praying for "a" man, but you are praying for "the" man God has appointed to lead, provide for, cover and protect you. Also, be sure to pray for your husband's children because you will need to love them as your own. If his children are left uncovered and Satan successfully launches an attack against them, he may delay your husband's arrival in your life. Know that

Satan will look for any and every opportunity to kill, steal and destroy what God has anointed and appointed to live and prosper. Intercede for your husband and come against every devil that's crazy enough to come against him.

Husband Interceptors

Understand this: Ishmael is a weapon formed against you. He is a weapon formed against your ministry, your husband, your womb, your children, your finances, your purpose and your peace. Even though he is a weapon formed against you, Ishmael does not look or feel like a weapon and that's why it is so easy for him to successfully carry out his assignment.

Attack Against Your Ministry: Ishmael is an attack against a woman's ministry because Satan sends him to distract her and lead her in the wrong direction. When this doesn't work, Satan will use an Ishmael to attack her ministry. Many of the women of God I've personally known and some of the women I've counseled have endured an attack from an Ishmael against their ministries. Of course, they'd married their Ishmaels and those men spent countless hours and days trying to convince their wives to disassociate from their churches, the people God has connected them with and their own God-given assignments. One of a husband's assignments is to lead his wife, but anything Satan sets up is perverted, meaning, it's rewired to do the opposite of what God designed it to do. An Ishmael's assignment is to pervert his wife's footsteps and ensure that she never rises up to be who she is called or chosen to be. If he is unsuccessful, many Ishmaels will seek to discredit their wives by spreading lies about them, spreading lies about their leaders, spreading lies about the churches they attend or by attempting to provoke their wives into doing something that would damage their good names. A good example of this would be a man who tries to fight his wife, but when she fights him back, he has her arrested.

Attack Against Your Husband: An Ishmael is sent to keep Isaac from finding his wife. You are a part of your God-ordained husband's assignment, and as such, you are a part of his ministry and purpose. Some Ishmaels don't come to keep a woman from doing what she's appointed to do, especially if her assignment is to simply help her husband with his assignment. They've come to intercept the husband's "good thing" and keep him from obtaining favor from God.

Attack Against Your Womb: Many women have been afflicted with infections and diseases by the men they've entrusted their bodies to. Some of them have even lost their ability to bear children. An Ishmael is an attack against a woman's womb in more ways than one. Through her womb, he creates sexual soul ties with her, which ensure that she cannot be found by her God-appointed husband until she's delivered and divorced in the realm of the spirit. Additionally, he creates children with her that he will not provide for, nurture, teach, lead nor protect. He creates children with her that she cannot provide for, and again, this discourages a woman from wanting to have any more children after she's struggled with the ones she's had with her Ishmael or Ishmaels. Because of him, many women have had tubal ligations to ensure that they could not have any more children. By doing so, they've closed off the passages between heaven and earth... passages God uses to send children through. God wanted to birth the children through them with the men who were assigned to them, but because of disobedience, many women have disabled their wombs to ensure that no more children are born through them.

Attack Against Your Children: Understand that just as God has assigned husbands to us, He has assigned children to us. Each person has a time stamp in which they are supposed to come into the realm of the earth and they have an assignment to complete in the earth. The earth is off balance spiritually because many of the men and women of God who were assigned to come into the earth were either aborted by their mothers or attacked by the men their mothers have chosen. Understand that God can and does use children born to the wrong men, and Satan knows this, so he sends weapons against those children in the form of romantic interests for their mothers. Many anointed and appointed children have been raped, molested, assaulted and even killed by the men their mothers invited into their lives.

Attack Against Your Finances: You have purpose, and with fulfilled purpose comes prosperity. One of Ishmael's assignments is to ensure that you are either financially dependent on him, the government or your family. In many cases, some Ishmaels come to depend on you financially. Satan understands that a saint outside of purpose is a saint whose finances are always open for attack.

Attack Against Your Purpose: Your purpose is your assignment in the realm of the earth. It is tied to your ministry, but it isn't necessarily the fullness of your ministry. Your purpose is whatever God has assigned you to do in the realm of the earth. It is the very heartbeat of your ministry and it is linked to your peace, prosperity and every facet of your life. An Ishmael's assignment is to distract you from your purpose, make sure you never come to the full knowledge of who you are in Christ and to pervert your purpose. Many Ishmaels want their wives or love interests to focus their attention only on their relationships with them. Their wives go to work, hang out with their Ishmael-approved friends and family members, go to bed and repeat the same cycle each and every day of their lives. They don't know who they are and they wouldn't dare venture outside of their Ishmael-approved schedules because Ishmael knows how to punish a woman who's outside of his will.

Attack Against Your Peace: Peace is a blessing from God and it is tied to our purpose and the fulfillment of our God-given assignments. Ishmael will always seek to keep any women tied to him from fulfilling their assignments by taking away their peace. One thing you will learn (if you haven't already learned) is that peace is as vital and as precious as the air we breathe. We oftentimes take our peace for granted until we lose it. It's something we don't think too much about until it's under attack.

Satan knows that we are creatures of adaption, and as such, we can find our own perverted versions of peace in any chaotic situations that we have adapted to. Once we've adapted to a lifestyle, it's hard for us to come outside of that lifestyle because when our comfort zones are removed, we're forced to face where we are in Christ. An Ishmael will always tear down the woman he's with, and then, create chaotic comfort zones for her to adapt to. He will reward her while she's in her demonically formed prison, and he will punish her every time she attempts to break out of her prison or she leaves its confines without his permission. Simply put, Ishmael will form himself as a woman's god and decide when she'll enter times of perverted peace and when she'll endure Ishmael-issued storms.

An Ishmael is a demonic interceptor designed to pervert the purpose of God in a woman's life. He is never the man who's easy to bypass; he is almost always that one who looks like Isaac, sounds like Isaac and appears to have the potential to someday become an Isaac.

Ishmaels don't always come after saved women either. Satan assigns them to women who have callings on their lives, even when they are in the world. He tries to intercept their husbands and ensure that they are the opposites of what and who God designed them to be. A good example is a man who came after me when I was deep in the world.

I was a young woman in the darkest hours of my sin. I was loving the sin that had enslaved me, but I was also coming to the realization that I could not continue living my life bouncing from one relationship to the next. I wanted to settle down with a guy. I wanted to get married and have children, so I became very attentive of the

men who pursued me. I was probably
around seventeen or eighteen years old
when a man from my neighborhood
approached me. *We'll call him William.* For
the last few years, he'd been pursuing me,
but I always turned him down. William was
between eight to ten years older than me
and I wasn't interested in older men. In
addition to him being older than me,
William had been a promiscuous man,
capitalizing on his good looks and smooth
words. He reminded me too much of one
of my dad's friends: a man who'd spent the
majority of his life being a womanizer who
saw women as nothing but tools for his own
selfish gratification.

When William approached me, he was
changed, but not in a good way. According
to William, he'd had an encounter with God
and he'd given his life over to the Lord.
Being demonically led myself, I knew
William's walk with God was bologna, but

for whatever reason, I allowed him to start visiting me. Honestly, I think I wanted to see how far William would go with his new profession; after all, he wasn't just claiming to have had an encounter with God, but William was suddenly walking around town toting a Bible and trying to minister to people. Nevertheless, he was infatuated with me, even claiming that God had told him that I was his wife.

At that stage in my life, I knew of God and I wanted to serve Him, but I didn't know how. My father had been a deacon for many years, but I had been introduced to the Lord in the wrong way: through religiousness. I saw most of the people who professed Christ as hypocrites with ulterior motives. Nevertheless, that didn't change my desire to have an authentic relationship with God, but I didn't know where to begin.

Of course, William tried to evangelize me,

but what was in me wanted to search out the sin in him. I know now that I was demonically led, or possibly even demonically possessed, but William's profession of faith had gotten my attention. Because of this, I stopped shutting the door in William's face anytime he came to visit. I stopped avoiding him and I started listening to him. Again, William was a very handsome man, but I saw him as a joke because he'd been a conceited womanizer with nothing more than his good looks to hold him up.

After William's alleged change, he claimed to have had many supernatural encounters with the Lord, including angelic encounters, levitating and so on. He would often talk about finding gold dust in his bathtub after taking a bath and I found his stories to be very amusing (and funny) because I wasn't saved. I had never heard of many of the things he spoke of. Nevertheless, I loved

that William was determined to make me
his wife. He even repeatedly told my
mother that I would someday be his wife,
and with me being a young woman, I'd
never seen a man behave the way he was
behaving. I kept telling him that I was in a
relationship with someone else, but I
wasn't. I liked William's company, but I did
not want him romantically because he was
weird (and old) to me.

One night, William came by our apartment
and we decided to go outside, sit in his car
and talk. Looking back, I can honestly say a
part of me wanted to see if there was any
possible way that I could even consider him
as a husband. I think one of the reasons I
hung around William was to see if he'd truly
changed, but something in me told me that
William was the same man singing a
different tune.

While we were seated in the car, William

began to speak about his angelic
encounters and all of the supernatural
things he claimed to have witnessed in the
last few months and days. We talked about
God and I shared my limited knowledge of
God with him, but something happened
that scared me to the core. While William
was talking, I'd looked over at him, but I
couldn't see the white of his eyes anymore.
I leaned closer as he spoke and realized that
his eyes were completely black. Startled, I
reached for the door handle, but I couldn't
take my eyes off William. I was moving
about frantically, and with that, William
looked over at me and asked what was
wrong. I'd taken my eyes off him for a few
seconds while I tried to free myself from his
car, but when I looked back at him, his eyes
were normal again. Now, understand that
I'd never had an encounter like that before,
nor was I in any way mentally deranged.
My heart was racing and I could barely
catch my breath. I explained to William

that his eyes had become very black and I
couldn't see the white of his eyes. William
then smiled at me and told me that one of
his relatives had experienced the same
thing while looking at him. While we were
talking, I turned away from him again, but
when I looked back at him, his eyes were
dark again. They were very, very dark and I
could not see the white in them at all.
Petrified, I tried to escape the car yet again,
but when I looked back at William, his eyes
were once again normal. That's when I
requested that we go into my mother's
apartment where there was light. That was
the first and only time that I had that
encounter, but nonetheless, it was an
encounter that I have never forgotten.

I tell this story to illustrate a point: Satan
always sends husband interceptors when
we're either ready for marriage or when we
think we're ready for marriage. Consider
these points:

- When William came to me toting a Bible, I'd just made up my mind that I wanted to get married and have children. William came to me claiming that God had told him that I was his wife. Satan knew that I was disgusted with William because of his womanizing, so when the enemy sent him after me, he came claiming to be a new man.
- I'd just started realizing that I needed a relationship with God, even though I didn't know where to begin. William came to me talking about God, miracles, signs and wonders. He knew how to get my attention.
- William came at a stage in my life where I was desperately trying to get my mother's approval. William's main focus was getting her approval of him because he knew that if my mother had told me to give him a chance, I would have.

Understand this: I was at a crossroads in my life and slowly, but surely, trying to find my way back to God. I was a lost soul, but I was also an anointed soul with an assignment and a God-appointed purpose and Satan knew this. In that hour of my life, Satan knew more about me than I did about myself, and that's what made it the darkest hour of my existence. Satan knew what type of weapon to form against me! While I'd convinced myself that I could never get involved with William, I was entertaining him because I wanted to see if William could change my mind about him. Again, he was a very handsome man, but even though I wasn't saved, I had the spirit of discernment in me. I always took a man's heart and saw it as his face, and because William had been a womanizer, I didn't see him as an attractive man. He was simply handsome, but he was not attractive. What's the difference? Being handsome was a fact that I couldn't get around, but I was not attracted to him, and therefore, he was not attractive to me. To me, he was an ugly man with a pretty face... nothing more.

Satan will send husband interceptors after you in accordance with who you are in Christ Jesus and where you are in Christ Jesus. When you're a babe, he'll send men who appear to be smarter or wiser than you. When you're a woman of God, meaning, you've grown up, he'll send men who appear to have the potential to be mighty men of God, men who aren't necessarily where you are in Christ. He does this because his goal is to pervert the order of marriage. Of course, he will sometimes send men who appear to be further than you are, but these men will be dark, Bible toting souls who've memorized scriptures and learned to look like men of God.

Some of the most popular husband

interceptors are exes because an ex is a man we're already familiar with.

Understand that Satan loves the familiar and that's why he assigns familiar spirits to people. Human beings are creatures of habit and adaption, and we feel safe in whatever comfort zones we've created for ourselves or we've been forced to live in. Consider some men in prison, for example. They've spent most of their lives there, so prison, for them, has become their comfort zones. Anytime they are released, they will commit a crime and intentionally leave evidence behind, hoping to get caught. Even though prison is not a desirable place to be, they've grown comfortable there. The point is... we oftentimes have comfort zones that are not God's best for us, but we stay there because we are afraid of change. For this reason, an ex makes for a great husband interceptor.

When an ex attempts to reenter a woman's

life, one of the first things he does is tell her that he's not the same man he once was. He does this to regain her trust and try to tear down the distorted image of himself that she has formed in her mind. Nevertheless, just because a man says he has changed doesn't necessarily mean that he has changed. Please know that anytime Satan sends an ex after you, he's sending a familiar spirit after you. He tries to reenter your life, and if you open that door, that familiar spirit will bring back seven spirits more evil than itself. That's why it's harder to get rid of an ex a second and third time than it was the first time.

Matthew 12:43-45 (ESV): When the unclean spirit has gone out of a person, it passes through waterless places seeking rest, but finds none. Then it says, 'I will return to my house from which I came.' And when it comes, it finds the house empty, swept, and put in order. Then it goes and brings with it seven other spirits more evil than itself, and they enter and dwell there, and the last state of that person is worse than the first. So also will it be with this evil generation."

A man sent to intercept your husband isn't always aware that he's on demonic assignment. Of course, not every man who tries to romantically link himself to you is on demonic assignment. Some of them are just mere men who see a woman they're interested in, but if they successfully enter your life, Satan will use them to intercept your husband, attack your purpose, pervert your thinking and chase away your peace. Some husband interceptors are true men of God who have good intentions for you, but they are not assigned to your life. Again, they aren't necessarily sent by Satan; sometimes, they're just men who see what they want and they choose to pursue it. Nevertheless, they can serve as husband interceptors, and it is not uncommon for a woman of God to romantically link herself to a man of God, only to have them be delivered from one another. The man may suddenly receive revelation knowledge that his fiance is not his God-appointed wife after courting her for three years. The same goes for the woman, but women aren't always receptive when their hearts are involved, so when it comes to matters of the heart, God oftentimes speaks to men.

We have to remain prayerful about any and every man who enters or attempts to enter our lives so that we don't waste time with any husband interceptors, be they demonically led or simply led of the flesh. We have purpose on the inside of us and everything and everyone assigned to us is tied to our purpose. We can't take relationships and courtships lightly. We need to remain prayerful and make sure we don't enter any sexual soul ties to ensure that we can clearly hear from God. This way, we don't waste our time with men who aren't our God-appointed husbands.

Anytime a man enters or attempts to enter your life, ask yourself (and God) who sent him. The evidence is oftentimes as plain as the nose on your face, but there are some men are who aren't so easily discerned. You will need to hear from the Lord regarding them, but you must be willing to hear from the Lord regarding them. Many women close their ears off to God when an Ishmael is saying everything they want to hear, but the Lord is telling them what they don't want to hear. Understand that there are many who have the potential to be your husband, but if you ask God to choose your husband for you, He will send the one He's already chosen for you, the one you're assigned to. He doesn't just have the potential to be your husband; he is your

God-appointed husband, assigned to you for such a time as this.

<u>Meeting God's Requirements</u>

Many women don't realize this, but God has
things He requires from all of us to reach
every season of our lives. Seasons are like
grade school. To get to the next level, you
must pass the level you're on, and just
because you look like you're ready for the
world doesn't necessarily mean you're
ready for it. Sometimes, we prematurely
ask God for things that we aren't quite
ready for; for example, if you're reading this
book, you've likely already asked the Lord
to send you a husband. You've asked for
"a" husband and not "your" husband
because you probably don't know who you
are in Christ Jesus. You weren't created to
be alone, so you want to fast-forward past
the seasons you're scheduled to walk
through and go straight into the season of

reaping. This is especially true if you believe you've obeyed God enough and sacrificed enough to get to the promised man. The truth is... you may be wife-ready, but that doesn't necessarily mean you're ready for the husband God has appointed for your life. Let me explain through an illustration.

Phyllis is a woman after God's own heart. She loves the Lord and she's been abstinent for the last four years. Phyllis has been praying for God to send her a husband and she's been reading up on a lot of literature about single living. Nevertheless, Phyllis waits another five years before she's found by her man of God. In total, she has had to wait nine years.

When Phyllis meets her husband, she better understands the reason she had to wait so long for the man she was assigned to. Her husband is a Prophet of God, a Pastor, an

Intercessor and a Prayer Warrior. He is a disciplined man who fasts twice a week, eats unprocessed foods and spends most of his time either in the sanctuary or in the streets evangelizing. Phyllis realizes that if God had sent her husband when she thought she was ready, she would not have been a good help meet for him. Four years before meeting Lawrence (her husband), Phyllis was not operating in her purpose or her ministry. She was simply a woman who loved God, feared God and went to church often. Sure, she was a faithful servant and a vessel of holiness, but the level of the man she was assigned to demanded that she walk at a level far removed from the level she was on. Had Phyllis met Lawrence when she thought she was ready, she would have served as a distraction, complained about the time and dedication he had to his assignment and she would have made her marriage to him all about herself. She would have seen Lawrence as her reward for being abstinent for four years, meaning, she did not yet possess the understanding she needed to accompany a mighty man of God. She needed to better understand who she was in the Lord, what she was purposed to do and she needed to be disciplined to ensure that she did not become a hindrance to her husband. Four years ago, Phyllis was ready to be married; that is a fact. But four years ago, Phyllis was not ready to be married to Lawrence.

You don't know what level of the anointing your husband is walking in, and that's why it is unwise for you to settle where you are in the Lord and start waiting for a husband. Some women would have been found years ago if they had simply come outside of their comfort zones and sought the Lord with their whole hearts. They simply got into a place that was far outside of where they used to be, and they began to compare where they were to where they used to be.

In doing so, many women became self-righteous, and from their pedestals of pride, they began to ask the Lord to send them husbands. Instead of husbands, God sent them through seasons designed to bring them out of pride and into His will. Please know that anytime you ask God for something, He has to first prepare you for what you've asked for before you can receive it. Sometimes, this place of preparation represents our very own wilderness experiences.

One of the worst things a wife-in-waiting can do is to stop preparing for her husband and start waiting for him. Your place of waiting is the place self-righteousness will oftentimes find you. You should never assume that you are where you're supposed to be in the Lord. Regardless of how far you've come and what you've left behind to get there, please know that there is always a greater level that can be reached. Oftentimes, it is the levels we are intimidated by that require us to come all the way outside of ourselves to reach the fullness of who we are in Christ Jesus. Sometimes, it's those levels that we are intimidated by that end up serving as the walls that stand between us and God. God wants us to come higher, but we think we've come high enough. God wants to reach deeper into our hearts and draw the deep rooted sin out of us, but we think He's reached deep enough. Sometimes, what God requires of us, we aren't requiring of ourselves. We are oftentimes silly enough to tell God that we are ready for our husbands when He begs to differ. Yes, we may be ready for "a" husband, but that doesn't necessarily mean we are ready for "the" appointed men of God who's assigned to our lives. The reality is that we have to meet God's expectations before we can expect to receive anything from Him.

At the age of sixteen, I found myself feeling left behind because most of my friends could drive. Because of this, I started putting a lot of pressure on my mother to teach me to drive, but she didn't have the patience to do so. I took a driver's education course at school, but that did nothing to help me learn how to drive. I simply learned the rules of the road, but I wasn't confident enough to stay on the road.

By the time I was seventeen, I'd learned to stay on the road and I'd gotten my driver's license. The truth is... I didn't past my driver's test; the man who gave me my driver's test was a big flirt and he passed me because I promised to call him (which, of course, I never did). Anyhow, after I got my license, my mother started letting me keep her car. She only required that I have a driver's license to keep it; the man who tested me only required that I call the

number he'd handed me to receive my
license, but the law required that I follow
the rules of the road while driving.
Needless to say, I learned to drive through
trial and error. By the time I got my license,
I'd learned to steer a car and stay on the
road, but truth be told, I should not have
been behind the wheel of anybody's car.
Because I wasn't truly ready, I ended up
backing into anywhere between three to
five cars, plus, I nearly flew across a railroad
track, and by the grace of God, I didn't
wreck the car, even though I did puncture
its radiator. I thought I was ready to drive,
but the law had expectations that were set
high enough to ensure that a reckless
person like me would not be licensed to kill
anyone. Nevertheless, I managed to get
around the law to get my license, and a lot
of people ended up paying for my
ignorance.

God has expectations of us, and even

though we've learned to steer ourselves to
church, read our Bibles and maintain our
purity, we may or may not be ready for the
man God has assigned us to. That is our
reality, but it is not a reason to become
anxious or frustrated; it should simply
motivate us to go further in the Lord. Many
women want God to spiritually license them
to become some man's wife, but they don't
have enough knowledge to keep them
married. You see, regardless of how God-
fearing a man is, he will have his own set of
issues. God does not connect imperfect
women with perfect men; He connects
imperfect women to imperfect men when
they are all connected to Him, a perfect
God. There have been many cases where a
wife has divorced her God-ordained
husband simply because she did not know
how to deal with his issues. It goes without
saying that his issues conflicted with her
issues, and the two had obviously come
together outside of their appointed seasons

or they came together in the right season with the wrong mindsets. When this happens, many couples end up marrying, divorcing, and then, remarrying one another once the Lord deals with them about their pride. They then go on to have powerful marriage ministries, helping young and old married couples overcome pride and connect to one another the right way. Many of the right people connect to one another the wrong way, so God has to shake them loose so they can reconnect in Him. God's expectations have to be met for us to have lifelong, God-protected marriages.

To meet God's expectations of you, you have to know the heart of God intimately. You can't just know of God and know that JEHOVAH is God; you need to know God on a personal level. You must learn to fear the Lord, and then, you must learn to love the Lord. Once you begin to fear God, you will

open yourself up for the wisdom of God.
Once you begin to get the wisdom of God,
you will learn to love Him all the more.
When you love Him, you'll seek to please
Him and you will learn to obey Him. Once
you begin to love God with all of your
might, He will begin to reveal your God-
purposed identity to you... an identity that
you need to meet, embrace and understand
before you are unveiled to your husband.
This means that you need to read your Bible
daily, pray often and seek the face of God
more than you're seeking a husband and a
paycheck. You need to become desperate
for the Lord to the point where you can't
sleep if you haven't spoken with Him. I
know this sounds far-fetched, but God
wants us to love Him with all of our
strength, our hearts and our might to
ensure that we don't enter any idolatrous
relationships with our husbands or any
other men. We have to taste and see that
the Lord is good before He releases us to be

our husbands "good things".

God's expectations of us may appear to be too high to reach, but they aren't. The hardest part is getting past ourselves, but once we make up our minds that we will serve the Lord regardless of what it costs us, the journey will then become easier. The hardest part of the journey is realizing that there is a price to pay, and this is sometimes a price we aren't willing to pay. However, once we understand that we will be required to make certain sacrifices to get to every blessing we've been crying out for, making those sacrifices won't be so difficult. Sometimes, we spend years wrestling with God, but when we stop resisting Him and we just let Him have His way in our lives, life becomes much easier. Women who aren't willing to make the necessary sacrifices oftentimes end up with the wrong men, and then, they are required to sacrifice far more than they would have if they had simply obeyed the Lord. When a woman refuses to meet God's expectations, she unknowingly agrees to meet Satan's expectations, which of course, are higher. She doesn't realize what she's agreeing to because Satan rarely shows the price tag of the sin; He simply advertises the benefits of the sin to us. It's very similar to a credit card advertisement. The credit card company will spend the majority of its commercial time advertising the benefits of having the card, and then, it will mention the interest fee as if it's a small price to pay. The company will not mention the hidden fees, including the annual and service fees. That's because it's a for-profit business. A credit card company's number one goal, just like any other business, is to earn money and stay in business. They aren't looking to benefit you, but they do know that having a credit card may benefit you from time-to-time. Even though the interest will not be for your benefit; it'll be for theirs. The point is... sin is not for you, even though it appears to have benefits. In the end, it'll cost you far more than you're willing to pay.

God requires that we walk in holiness, shunning the things that He hates and embracing the things that He loves. He wants to reveal a lot about Himself to us, and He wants to reveal to us a lot about ourselves, but we've got to be willing to receive this knowledge. We have to be willing to make the necessary sacrifices, which includes, but are not limited to:

- The ending of certain familiar relationships (family).
- The ending of certain friendly relationships.
- Disconnecting from certain people in the church, or disconnecting from certain churches. Understand that just because it has "church" in its name doesn't mean that God attends

it or tends to it. Some churches are buildings where demons assemble and learn to look like saints.

- Connecting to people we may have little to nothing in common with.
- Walking away from jobs and opportunities that go against God's plans for us.
- Leaving cities, states, and sometimes, the country you are in to embrace your assignment in Christ Jesus.
- Giving up personal possessions (sometimes money) so that God can restart our lives and build our faith.
- Walking away from the people we are romantically involved with or rejecting the people who we are interested in and have the opportunities to be romantically involved with. Sometimes, we have to turn down good ideas to embrace the God ideas.
- Being brought outside of our comfort

zones to embrace new mindsets, new levels and new opportunities.

Let's face it. We require a lot from God. It is silly to think that we can expect so much from Him and that He should not expect anything from us in return. God doesn't ask for much, but what He asks for can cost us everything. Nevertheless, anything that God removes from our lives is the price we pay to receive what God wants to add to our lives, which of course, is far more valuable than what He removed.

Ask the Lord what He expects of you, and then, seek to fulfill His expectations. Seek to please the Lord in every way, and when you seek the whole heart of God, He will reveal to you His plans for you.

1 Corinthians 2:9 (KJV): But as it is written, Eye hath not seen, nor ear heard, neither have entered into the heart of man, the

things which God hath prepared for them
that love him.

<u>When You're Not Ready to be Found</u>

Just about every woman-in-waiting thinks she's ready to be found by her God-appointed husband, but the truth is only wives-in-waiting are ready to take on their new roles. Here's the thing: God never said that a man who finds a woman finds a good thing and obtains favor from the Lord. He said that "he who finds a wife finds a good thing and obtains favor from the Lord". This means that a wife is hidden, but women are easy to come by. Before a woman becomes a wife-in-waiting, she goes through a process of dying to herself, obtaining wisdom, knowledge and understanding, and she learns what the role she's applying for entails. The average woman thinks marriage is just two people living together, sharing the bills, having legal sex, and labeling one another as their spouse. But there's more to marriage than meets the eye. With God, marriage is a united front that not only mirrors our relationship with Him, but teaches us more about our relationship to Him. Marriage is ministry. It is not a divided front where two selfish people come together and fight over who's going to be in charge; it is a united front where two selfless people come together (in the Lord) and take their God-instituted positions.

Marriage isn't a cure for loneliness or a lifetime prescription to legal sex. It is not a union for two incomplete people to try and complete one another; it is a union where two whole people come together as one person in the name of our Lord and Savior, Jesus Christ.

Matthew 18:20: For where two or three have gathered together in My name, I am there in their midst.

When I got married the first time, I was new to the church scene, fresh out of the world and still carrying myself like the world. Sin was what I knew, so I sinned my way into marriage. To me, marriage was all about me, but since God said that sex outside of the covenant of marriage was a sin, I wanted to get married so I wouldn't be in sin. Because I'd entered marriage with the wrong mind and wrong heart, I entered marriage with the wrong man. Like most couples, we got along for the most part, but when we fought, we fought hard. To him, marriage was all about him. He was self-centered, self-righteous and selfishly motivated. He was a wounded soul who saw women as creatures who were predisposed to do evil, so I ended up paying for the mistakes of many of my predecessors. At the same time, he paid for the mistakes of many of his predecessors because I saw men as creatures who needed to be kept on a tight leash to ensure they didn't cheat. It goes without saying, the two of us fought a lot, and our marriage eventually gave way.

When I married for the second time, I can't say that I was a babe in Christ. I was more of a teenager in Christ, meaning, I knew that fornication was wrong, but I rebelled against the Word. I knew that God wanted me to present my body as a living sacrifice, holy and acceptable onto Him, but I didn't know how to be holy. I didn't have enough wisdom to keep me or enough love for God to convict me, so I fornicated my way back to the altar yet again. I used to think that I could give God what He required of me after I got what I wanted. I would fulfill the lusts of my flesh, and then, my guy and I would make our way to a nearby

courthouse and make our sex legal in the
eyes of God. After that, I would bring my
sinner-men into the church so they too
could get saved, sanctified and filled with
the Holy Spirit. I thought I simply needed to
get them into a deliverance ministry where
the minister would lay eyes on them, see
the demons hiding in them, and then, cast
those demons out. I would then take my
prized husband back to the house and we
would live happily ever after. Of course,
that did not happen. I learned the hard way
that you can't sin your way into a blessing. I
learned the hard way that when God gives
people free will, He gives them the ability to
choose what they want to do and who they
want to serve.

As I continued to grow in the Lord, I noticed
that I kept outgrowing the men I'd chosen
for myself. In the first marriage, I'd grown
up quite a bit, and the closer I got to God,
the further away I got from him. In the

second union, the Lord stripped me of the ignorance and lack of knowledge that once allowed me to call myself a babe, and He grew me up (suddenly and without warning) into a woman of God. When God stripped away the flesh and filled me with His supernatural wisdom, knowledge and understanding, I immediately realized that I'd chosen the wrong man for myself. It was then that I had to learn to pray more, fast more and complain less. Both marriages turned out to be miserable unions because I'd gotten married while I was still self-righteous and prideful, so the men I chose for myself were a reflection of who I once was. My crime against them was that I kept trying to change them. I tried to win their souls for Christ, but my motivation for doing so was purely selfish. I was not ready for marriage either time, and because of this, I ended up marrying the wrong men. With that being said, I could not and cannot blame them for being who they were

because I met and married them in the very
condition that they were in when I divorced
them. They hadn't suddenly changed on
me; I changed on them. I started growing
closer to the Lord and I became less and
less of the woman they'd fallen for. That's
because I didn't know who I was when I met
them, but as God revealed His heart to me
and began to show me my identity, I could
no longer relate to the men I'd chosen for
myself.

As I grew in the Lord, I began to understand
the stages of growth and why God won't
send us husbands when we're petitioning
heaven for them. Your husband has to find
you in a certain mindset, which means that
he would also be in that mindset. Where a
husband finds his wife is oftentimes the
mindset he'll attempt to settle down in.
That's why we have to seek the kingdom of
God and all God's righteousness first, and
then, let Him add everything else to us. He

wants us to be kingdom-minded when we get married; that way, when we settle down with our husbands, we'll settle down in a kingdom-mindset.

I get a lot of messages from women who say that they've been waiting on God for their husbands for years, and they can't figure out why God is making them wait so long. Many of these women believe they've done everything God required of them, but God still hasn't released them to be found. Below are ten of the main reasons I've found that God keeps His daughters hidden:

1. **They aren't ready to be found yet-** Sometimes, we think we're ready, but we're basing our beliefs on how far we've come and how much we've been delivered from. Just because you're abstinent and prayerful doesn't mean that you're ready to be found. God determines when we're ready and He looks at the hidden

142

places of our hearts to determine if
we are ready to be help meets.

2. **They don't know their identities in
the Lord yet-** This has got to be the
number one reason most single
women aren't found yet. You must
know your identity in the Lord before
you can help someone else with their
assignment. What were you put in
the realm of the earth to do? You
need to know this before God labels
you a wife-in-waiting.

3. **They aren't seeking the kingdom of
God first and foremost-** This is the
second reason most single women
end up waiting for years on end. God
requires that He be number one in
our lives, and this rearranging of our
priorities isn't something we can do
overnight. It's a process of tearing
down self, reading the Word of God
everyday and spending intimate time
in the presence of God daily. You'll

know when God takes the number one spot in your heart because you'll begin to start each day with Him and you won't be so anxious to get married. You will find yourself content with the Lord, but this doesn't mean that you won't desire a husband. It simply means that you won't be overly-anxious to have one.

4. **They are not yet ready to be "their" husband's help meet-** They're wife-ready, but they are not ready for the husbands God has assigned them to. Again, you have to be dressed and prepared for the husband God chose for you according to the level and mantle he's walking in.

5. **They keep dating every man who looks promising to them-** God told us to be anxious for nothing, but the truth is, the average woman-in-waiting is anxious to be found by her husband or a husband. Because of

this, the average woman-in-waiting will, at minimum, go out to eat and exchange her phone number with any and every man who peaks her interest. The solution? Don't be average. Some Ishmaels are as plain as the nose on your face. Remember, you are waiting for your God-sent husband and you should not waste your time entertaining the ones Satan sends. Women who date, court and hang out with every man or just about every man who entertains their eyes, always end up putting off their seasons of expectancy by years, and sometimes, decades.

6. **They're still connected to or contacting their exes-** It is not uncommon to see a woman who's still engaging with one or more of her exes. In many of these cases, such a woman may not have direct contact with the ex, but she will stay

connected to his family so that she can know his every move. Sure, she says that she's simply friends with the family and she should not have to cut them off just because he was a huge jerk, but the truth of the matter is... she is still soul tied to him. She wants him back and she wants to make sure that she has his family's backing. Nevertheless, such a woman will get on her knees and ask God to send her a husband once she begins to realize that her ex isn't going to come around anytime soon. Of course, God won't send her appointed husband to her because she's still married in the realm of the spirit to her ex and she doesn't want a divorce.

7. **They're still soul tied, or better yet, illegally married to someone else-** You don't have to be in contact with your ex or your ex's family to still be

soul tied to him. The truth is... the
average woman is soul tied to one or
more men, and because of this, they
often go year after year being
women-in-waiting, rather than being
wives-in-waiting. This means that
they cannot and will not be found
until their statuses change in the eyes
of the Lord. How do you divorce
every man you've tied yourself to?
It's simple. Ask God to divorce you
from them, and then, make sure you
remain disconnected from them in
every sense of the word. Don't call
their family members, don't visit their
social media pages and don't talk
about them unless you're testifying
about what God brought you
through. In other words, a wife-in-
waiting has to behave like a wife
who's waiting for her husband to
return home. She cannot behave like
a single woman; she must carry

herself as if she's already been found.

8. **They're still connected to the people or churches God has told them to disconnect from-** The truth is... we have all been delivered from something or need deliverance from something. We watch in awe as people get delivered from demons all the time, but the average believer doesn't realize that we also have to be delivered from people with demons and churches where demons assemble. Every one who cries "Lord, Lord" will not enter heaven, and this means that not everyone who calls themselves Christians are saved. With that being said, a lot of believers are connected to the wrong people simply because they have not prayed about their connections. Instead, the enemy binds people with people. Some people have the accents of heaven, but they don't

speak the language of heaven,
meaning, they know how to sound
like the saints of God, but they are in
no way God's children. So, for
example, one woman may bind
another woman by taking her to
dinner, paying her electric bill and
helping her to get back on her feet.
The woman who's been helped may
feel obliged to remain connected to
the woman who helped her, not
understanding that God said to owe
no man anything but to love him.
Nevertheless, God speaks to the
bound woman and tells her to
disconnect from the woman who's
binding her. He even sends her the
money she needs to pay back her
slavemaster so that she can serve
Him the right way, but she uses that
money to pay off some bills. In such
a case, she has blocked herself from
receiving the blessings of God,

including her God-appointed husband. God doesn't want us depending on anyone for anything, and He definitely doesn't want us owing anyone anything.

9. **They are not guarding their hearts-** The Bible tells us to guard our hearts, for out of it flows the issues of life. What does it mean to "guard your heart"? It's simple. The heart, biblically speaking, is your mind. God is saying to be careful what you allow into your mind. The mind has several levels, with the first level being the conscious mind. The conscious mind is activated by what we are presently seeing, hearing or experiencing at any given moment. Anything that we watch on television, listen to on the radio or experience live is engaging our conscious minds. Your conscious mind is what you are presently aware of. Everything that you allow into

your conscious mind is auditioning
for a place in your subconscious
mind. It does this through a series of
imaginations, and that's why God told
us to cast down imaginations and
every high thing that exalts itself
against the knowledge of God. Our
imaginations are the "waiting rooms"
of our subconscious minds, and they
determine what we allow to enter
the next level of our hearts, or better
yet, our minds. In order for us to let
something into our subconscious
minds, we must first believe it, and
that's why our imaginations are
important to Satan. It is in the
outskirts of our minds that he
campaigns the hardest, showing us
the desires and lusts of our hearts,
and then, promising that we can have
whatever it is that we are desiring or
coveting by sinning against God. If
we allow ourselves to watch or listen

to media that is ungodly, it will
eventually scale our conscious minds
and make its way into our
subconscious minds. The
subconscious mind is pretty much
your memory. It is what you have
given place to in your heart. It is the
part of the mind that drives you and
it is the part of the mind that Satan
usually accesses the most. Lastly,
there is our unconscious mind, which
is the hardest part to be accessed. It
is the part of our minds that control
our breathing and instinctual
behaviors. Of course, this is the part
of the mind that Satan wants to
access the most because it is there
that he can stop a person from
breathing, cause them to believe that
they cannot walk or function in their
bodies or shut down the very
instincts we need to survive. A
woman who does not guard her heart

is a woman who Satan has easy access to. Because of this, the Lord won't release her to be any man's wife until she learns to guard her heart. In other words, if the music goes against the Word of God, don't listen to it. If the media promotes sin, don't watch it. If the people aren't living holy lifestyles, don't connect with them. Make sure your heart is constantly fed the Word of God and you are always in the presence of God's people. The only time you are to be in the company of ungodly people is when you are telling them about God and trying to win their souls for the kingdom.

10. **They are celibate fornicators**- A while back, the Lord gave me this powerful term and He said to me that many of His daughters are celibate fornicators. What they do is close their legs and try to manipulate Him

into sending husbands to them
through their works, but their minds
have not changed. Many of them
take vows of abstinence or celibacy
because they've sinned with several
men, only to realize that none of
those men were willing to marry
them. So, they came across some
woman who was practicing
abstinence or they heard their
preachers preach about purity and
they decided to use abstinence as a
tool to pressure God into sending
husbands to them. Their motives
aren't right and they have not given
God the number one place in their
hearts. Secretly, they still worship
the idea of marriage and they still
idolize men. Nevertheless, they go to
church, speak Christian words and
declare their purity to anyone who
will hear them. Many of them don't
realize it, but they are attempting to

154

mock God. How so? They are openly testing God by promoting their works, and then, trying to force God into giving them the lusts of their hearts. When they don't receive the husbands they've been praying for, many of these women will openly commit blasphemy and they will directly or indirectly attempt to discourage other women from practicing purity. They'll say things like, "I was abstinent for seven years and God didn't send me a husband! One of my friends wasn't abstinent and she is now married to an amazing man. After seven years of waiting, I went out and found my own man and we are still together to this day!" Their hearts were never in submission to God and what they won't openly share with you is the true state of the relationships they are in. They won't tell you that the men they're living with or married to are mentally, verbally and physically abusive. They won't tell you that the men they are publicly boasting about are cheating on them. They are women who are angry with God because He would not be manipulated by them. Many women-in-waiting are taking this very same path! They are testing God, rather than taking Him at His Word. The difference is that someone who tests God doesn't believe Him, but someone who takes Him at His Word believes Him and seeks to glorify Him.

When you're not ready to be found, God will not release your husband to find you. Instead, He will charge you to seek His face all the more. Women who are not ready to be found are usually:

1. **Financially Dependent-** They want to depend on a man to pay their bills.

They see husbands as double blessings, whereas, they can enjoy endless rounds of legal sex, all the while, not having to worry about their bills.

2. **Emotionally Dependent-** Emotionally dependent women usually surround themselves with other people because they've attributed their value to the amount of people around them or the quality of the people around them.

3. **Soul Tied-** They have yet to truly repent of their fornications, and because of this, they are still soul tied to the men in their past.

4. **Full of Strife or Unforgiveness-** They are still mad at some man because he left them or betrayed them.

5. **Religious-Minded-** Religious-minded people perform a bunch of works, thinking their works will move God. Heaven-minded people obey God

because they love and fear Him. The difference is... one performs while the other demonstrates.

If you're not ready to be found by your husband, you are in the perfect place to hear from the Lord.

1 Corinthians 7:33-34 (ESV): And the unmarried or betrothed woman is anxious about the things of the Lord, how to be holy in body and spirit. But the married woman is anxious about worldly things, how to please her husband.

Utilize this time to get closer to God. You will be glad you did because the more you get to know God, the more content you'll be with Him. You will discover truths about God that will make you want to know Him all the more. You will learn more about yourself and what God has placed in you. Once you truly start this journey, you will begin to experience the joy, contentment and peace of God. If you have not experienced this yet, you are not ready to be a wife, but that's okay. You simply need to take this time out to experience God like you've never experienced Him before. Below are three steps to having a more intimate relationship with God:

1. **Read your Bible daily-** Sure, reading the Bible is hard at first, but once you make a habit of it, it won't be so difficult. Remember, it takes 17-21 days to establish a habit. The easiest way to start a habit is to schedule yourself to do something. Schedule some time every night or every morning to read a chapter in your Bible. Make sure that the version of the Bible you are reading from is one you understand. The way the human mind is setup is... we will read the words that we don't comprehend, but we won't, by default, seek to

understand them. That's why it's never a great idea to read a version of the Bible that you don't understand. Nowadays, there are many translations of the Bible that are easily understood by modern man. Pray and ask the Lord which version you should read, and also, check out some Bible websites to see which versions read better to you. The most popular versions outside of the King James Bible, include the New International Version (NIV), New Living Translation (NLV), English Standard Version (ESV), the New American Standard Bible (NASB) and the American King James Version (AKJV).

2. **Spend time in prayer daily-** You may not think that God hears you, but He does. The first level of prayer is usually the one that feels awkward because your carnal mind will try to

reason with you. It'll ask you questions like, "Why are you praying to a God you cannot see?" However, the more time you spend talking to God, the more you will come to believe that He is real and that He is with you.

3. **Let God choose your Pastor-** Understand this: Not every man or woman who claims to love and fear the Lord actually loves and fears the Lord. One of the greatest mistakes many believers make today is choosing their own Pastors. This crime is even more dangerous than choosing your own husband. Pray about the leaders you have and ask God to send you to the church (building) that He wants you to be a part of. Ask Him to send you where His Holy Spirit is welcome. Don't be alarmed at where He sends you. Sometimes, He will take you out of a

large church and send you to a small,
barely developed church.
Sometimes, He will take you out of a
small church and send you into a
large church. God doesn't care about
the size of the ministry. What's
important to Him is that He is
welcome in that ministry.

Let God build on your relationship with Him
and anytime you find yourself becoming
overly anxious, pray and ask the Lord to
give you peace. The beauty in this is that
even though you may not be ready to be
found, if you continue seeking God, you will
find Him and He will declare you a wife-in-
waiting before you know it. Some women
end up waiting decades because they would
not submit their whole hearts to God;
instead, they chose religion over God.
Nevertheless, you don't have to be like
them. You simply need to seek His face,
even when it doesn't make sense to your

carnal mind or the carnal-minded people around you. Keep on seeking the Lord and let Him show you how good He is. Once you allow Him to have His way in your heart and life, He will declare you to be a wife, and that's when He will release your husband to find you. Don't be more determined to be a wife than you are to be a daughter of the King of kings and Lord of lords.

Preparing to be Found

I'm about to tell you to do something that will offend religious thinking and challenge the very title of this book. Stop waiting on your God-ordained husband to find you. The average woman waits for her God-appointed husband, but a wife-in-waiting isn't sitting around waiting for her husband to find her. She is preparing to be found. Therefore, I say to you to stop waiting and start preparing. The word "waiting" is a passive word that implies you're doing nothing, but the word "preparing" is an action word that implies that you have the faith needed to receive whatever it is that you're preparing for. Sure, if God has a husband selected for you, you are, in a sense, waiting for him to find you, but the wait should not be intentional. It's simply the state you're in, but it's not your state of mind. Think about it this way: You board a plane that's supposed to be heading to China. The plane is supposed to take off at 2:30 that afternoon, but it is delayed because of the weather. At 2:35, the pilot announces that he is waiting to receive the clearance to take off. An hour later, he makes the same announcement. A day later, he makes the same announcement. Can you truly say you're on your way to China? Not at all. You're waiting for take-off. Once the plane gets off the ground, you can then say you're on your way to China. Nevertheless, your wait isn't intentional; it's not your fault. There's nothing you can do to make that plane take off any sooner, so you sit in your seat and wait. You do know, however, that the plane will eventually take you to China, so you have no choice but to stay seated until the pilot receives clearance for take-off.

Many women who say that they are waiting for their husbands are basically saying that they aren't doing anything new. They are following their monotonous life's schedules, but they've added a little purity to the mix in hopes that God will send them the husbands they've been praying for. Nevertheless, the Bible tells us that faith without works is dead. It isn't in a coma and it isn't paused; it's dead, lifeless, nonexistent. God loves the Word because He is the Word but the Word has to be applied, meaning, we have to do something that confirms that we believe God.

It was the end of 2013 and I had recently separated from my second husband. Of course, like any other woman in that situation, I was hurt, angry and ashamed. I understood my divorce. I'd met and married a man while I was still a spiritual teenager and I'd grown up while married to him. I didn't initiate the divorce; I simply stood still and let everything happen. I let the unbeliever depart, just as God instructs us to do in His Word. Nevertheless, the hurt, anger and shame I felt was overshadowed by a joy I didn't completely understand. A part of me questioned whether it was good for me to feel the way I was feeling, but I knew in my heart that God was delivering me. I knew that God was giving me another chance and I had committed to Him and myself that I would not fail this time. After all, I was no longer a babe in Christ. I could no longer justify going after unsaved men, and then, trying to drag them into the church.

I embraced my new reality and I grieved my loss. I allowed myself to feel whatever I needed to feel, and anything that was ungodly, I laid it at the feet of God and repented of it. I asked the Lord to deliver me from unforgiveness; that way, I wouldn't become a snare to myself and others. God gave me the love and understanding I needed to forgive my ex-husband and He taught me to take accountability for my part in our divorce. We were divorcing because we should have never gotten married. We were divorcing because we were *extremely* unequally yoked. We were divorcing because I'd finally chosen God over myself and others. I began to serve the Lord with all of my heart, mind and soul, and my love for Him went far outside of my comprehension. I stopped trying to make marriage all about me and I started honoring, loving and submitting to the husband I'd chosen for myself. It was then that I better understood James 4:7, which reads, "Submit yourselves therefore to God. Resist the devil, and he will flee from you." I'd given the Lord my whole life and my heart, and I'd chosen Him over the last few years of that marriage consistently and without fail. I'd grown up and I was not about to put a man or myself

before the Lord anymore. So, I began to
serve God like never before, and God began
to use me all the more.

I didn't understand it then, but before my
ex and I broke up, the Lord began to
minister to me, telling me to do things by
myself, for myself. Before then, I felt like I
needed my husband to be with me
everywhere I went. I wouldn't eat out by
myself. I complained if I had to walk by
myself, and I loathed every trip my ex
would make. I was too dependent on the
man, and God delivered me from that
dependency. What I learned is that we
often marry people when we have voids,
and they marry us because they like the fact
that we are so dependent on them. In a
sense, we make idols of them and a broken
man loves to know that he is worshipped in
one way or another. Howbeit, when God
delivers us from those voids, we are forced
to get to know our spouses at a level we

never sought to know them. When this
happens, we realize that we can no longer
walk together because we are not in
agreement with one another.

I was sad about the divorce, but excited at
the same time. I was excited about the
opportunity to practice what I'd preached.
God had been using me to warn single
women, and He had me to use my
testimony as a warning shot. I'd grown
passionate about purity and my love for
God was stable.... truly stable. Knowing
that I was about to practice purity was
exciting to me, as weird as that sounds. I
wanted to experience God on a whole new
level, and I knew that I could finally position
myself to be found by the man God
appointed for me. I didn't have to be
bound to the husband of disobedience
anymore. I could prepare for the appointed
one.

What I didn't realize was that by serving the Lord in my failed marriage, I was learning to be the daughter God had designed me to be and the wife my God-appointed husband would someday find. In the last year of my marriage to my ex, I was the best wife I'd ever been in my life. I'd learned to be submissive and non-argumentative. I stopped trying to pressure my then-husband into serving the Lord, and I just started demonstrating my love and fear of the Lord. I'd been doing this our entire marriage, but in the last year, I was fully and incurably in submission to God. Of course, this is confusing to some people because many would question why we got divorced if I had become a better servant of God and a better wife. My ex hadn't married me for the right reason and I had to come to terms with that. He was a foreign man who dreamed about living in America. His dream had finally come true, and I had to really stop lying to myself and allow myself to see what I didn't want to see. He did not love me and I could no longer deny it, but regardless of that, I still served as his wife in a way that would make the Lord proud. One day, he left, and a few days later, he filed for divorce, and I was okay with that. I wanted to be loved... truly loved and not just tolerated.

Regardless of what I was going through, the Lord still managed to make me smile. I tried not to meditate on where I was, but more so where the Lord was taking me. I saw my impending divorce as my final shot at doing things the right way. I could take God at His Word and finally live the life I'd been teaching others to live.

During that time, the Lord began to show me how many qualities He birthed in me during my marriage... qualities that I had been missing when my ex and I had initially married. I'd gotten married with a woman's mindset, but not with the heart of a wife. Nevertheless, within the first year of that marriage, God had opened my eyes and began to teach me to be a wife. It took several years for me to understand my role, but once I better understood it, I was able to apply it. I saw the changes in me. I became more organized, even though I was already somewhat organized. I became more loving and less argumentative. I became more patient and less dependent. I truly became a help meet, often volunteering to take on the projects and financial responsibilities that my ex seemed to be intimidated by. I became a wife who encouraged her husband and I learned to speak blessings over the man I was married to. I didn't realize it, but I became a wife. I was no longer merely a married woman; I became a genuine, God-fearing wife. Because of this, the man I married had come to a crossroads with God. He had to choose God and keep me or reject God and

lose me. By the time our divorce was
finalized, I was already a wife-in-waiting.

After my ex and I divorced, God began
sending many Prophets my way and they
prophesied of the husband He had for me.
That's when I realized that I couldn't simply
wait on the man of God; I needed to be
prepared for him. After all, he's not an
ordinary man of God. He is an
extraordinary man of God... a man who
fears the Lord with all of his heart and
might. Being anointed wasn't enough... I
needed to put that anointing to work all the
more and learn how to become "his" wife
and not just "a" wife-in-waiting. So, I began
to pray about my husband and ask God to
ready me for him. In this chapter, I will
teach you what God taught me.

Some of the things I learned to do included:
1. Building good habits and tearing
   down the bad ones. This act is

intentional and it has to be something you work at daily. For example, I stopped leaving empty toilet paper rolls in the bathroom. I started replacing any and everything I used, including paper towels and toothpaste. Before then, I would simply replace toilet paper whenever I needed it. I didn't realize how bad of a habit this was until God made me confront it.

2. I started stocking up on my household necessities, instead of waiting until they were low or gone to replace them. Nowadays, for example, I normally buy two, 12 count packages of paper towels and two, 24 count packages of toilet paper. I tend to buy two or more of everything and I don't wait for any of my supplies to be low before I replace them.

3. I got rid of unnecessary expenses. I

wasn't watching cable television, so I got rid of it. I also got rid of my home phone service and replaced it with a cheaper alternative.

4. I learned to be more organized. Again, I was already an organized woman, but I learned to be even more organized. Even though I'm really organized now, I still seek to become better.

5. I started paying my bills as soon as I got them. When I was married to my ex, he paid most of the bills, but before we were married, I was a woman who avoided and delayed paying bills. I'd learned from my ex the importance of paying bills speedily, so when we broke up, I continued to pay off my monthly bills as soon as I received them.

6. I worked on rebuilding my credit. Over the years, my credit score rose from 450 to 700. Of course, I was

happy about this, but I wanted to make sure that I didn't return to the Tiffany I once was, so I started looking for long lost, unpaid bills. I paid off every bill that came my way and it felt great to finally be a responsible woman. Again, I had finally grown up.

7. I worked harder at building my business. Growing up, I somehow learned that a man's responsibility was to take care of me. Because of this belief, I didn't go to college, nor did I try to do anything to better my own life. I simply worked and waited for some man to come along, blend his money with mine and make my life easier. This changed when I was going through my first divorce. My ex and I had recently separated and we were on the phone arguing. He left to be with someone else, and he was upset with me because I wouldn't

accept our new living arrangements. I was passionate about not being cheated on, and he knew I wasn't going to sit around and wait for him to return home. Because of this, he said to me that I was going to lose my house, my car and everything I had. In other words, he was saying that he would no longer pay any of the bills in that house, and because all of our bills required two incomes to be maintained, I was about to lose it all. It was in that moment that something clicked on the inside of me, and I said in my heart that I would never depend on a man again. I made sure I lived up to my new proclamation when I was married the second time, even though he didn't require that I pay any bills except the cell phone bill and buy groceries every other week. Nevertheless, I loved being able to help, so I stored up money, and

anytime a large expense came about
or whenever he felt overwhelmed, I
would happily run to the rescue. It
wasn't long before I realized that I
loved being a help to my husband. I
had truly become a help meet.
Nowadays, I'm not afraid to lean on
my God-appointed husband (when I
meet him), but I want the joy of
knowing that I'm not a weight on him
and I can help him when he needs it.
I learned that when you depend on
anyone but God, He will teach you
that man is not dependable, but
when you depend on God, He will
send you a husband who depends on
Him as well. You can lean on a man
who is wise enough to lean on God.

8. I stopped being an over-spender and I
started looking for ways to invest my
money, or better yet, sow seeds. I
learned the principal of sowing and
reaping, so I started sowing into

fertile ground. That way, when my husband finds me, he doesn't just find his wife, but he finds his Proverbs 31 woman. When my husband finds me, he will know what favor is because he won't just reap a wife, he will reap of what his wife has sown.

9. I learned the power of connections and the freedom of disconnecting. In our lives, we are going to have many God-appointed connections, just as we will connect to people who make sense to us. Nevertheless, a carnal connection has enough power to ruin a God-appointed connection. With that knowledge in tow, I began to pray about people and ask the Lord to remove any and everyone who He had not sent into my life and to remove any and everyone whose season in my life had expired.

10. I learned to truly intercede for my

husband. When I was married the first and second time, I prayed for my husbands, but I didn't know the power of interceding for them. Praying for them is one thing, but intercession is better. Praying entails me asking the Lord to give them what I thought they deserved and to deliver them from any mindsets or people who I believed endangered our marriage. Interceding entails me asking the Lord to deliver my husband from anything and everyone who is not like Him. Intercession involves warfare and standing in the gap for a man who may not deserve another chance. I learned to intercede on behalf of my second ex, but when our marriage ended, God taught me a greater level of intercession. I began to intercede for my God-appointed husband, often standing in the gap for him. I also learned to recognize an Ishmael for what it was... an attempted attack against the marriage that God had appointed for me. Because of this, I rejected many men, and the two who got my number were sent away days after exchanging numbers with me. I didn't want to put another man in my husband's place. I am my husband's crown; I am one of his many blessings and I had to behave as such to be found by him.

Preparing to be found is a faith move. It means that you believe God above what you have been taught, tasted or experienced. It means that your faith is not found in the natural realm, but that you are believing for what you cannot see. Many women claim they are ready, but please know this: You will be tested according to your own words! An Ishmael will come along who meets almost everything on your wishlist for a husband. He may even supersede your expectations. He will be almost everything you've been praying for, and you will not want to send him away. It takes faith to send an Ishmael away because in doing so, you are proving that you believe God for your Isaac.

Again, an Ishmael is not a man who is easily sent away. Some guys don't look, speak or behave like the promised man, and therefore, they are not Ishmaels. They are mere jokes, but amazingly enough, some of them do get the girl. A true Ishmael comes after a woman who has truly been waiting for her appointed man of God... a woman who has forsaken her "type" of man and rejected many of the men Satan has sent her way. An Ishmael is designed to stop the promise from coming to pass. His assignment is to distract, derail and destroy. An Ishmael rarely comes after a woman-in-waiting because she's distracted by mere men. An Ishmael is assigned to intercept a wife-in-waiting.

More than fifty percent of the wives-in-waiting have fallen into the arms of an Ishmael because they forgot to stop waiting and start preparing. If you don't prepare, you won't be ready. If you're not ready, you'll miss your appointed season.

Matthew 25:1-13 (NIV): At that time the kingdom of heaven will be like ten virgins who took their lamps and went out to meet the bridegroom. Five of them were foolish and five were wise. The foolish ones took their lamps but did not take any oil with them. The wise ones, however, took oil in jars along with their lamps. The bridegroom was a long time in coming, and they all became drowsy and fell asleep. "At midnight the cry rang out: 'Here's the bridegroom! Come out to meet him!' "Then all the virgins woke up and trimmed their lamps. The foolish ones said to the wise, 'Give us some of your oil; our lamps are going out.'

" 'No,' they replied, 'there may not be enough for both us and you. Instead, go to those who sell oil and buy some for yourselves.'

"But while they were on their way to buy the oil, the bridegroom arrived. The virgins who were ready went in with him to the wedding banquet. And the door was shut.

"Later the others also came. 'Lord, Lord,' they said, 'open the door for us!'

"But he replied, 'Truly I tell you, I don't know you.'

"Therefore keep watch, because you do not know the day or the hour."

One of the lines in this parable that stood out the most to me was: *The bridegroom was a long time in coming, and they all became drowsy and fell asleep.* How many wives-in-waiting become weary after having waited a long time for their appointed men of God to find them? The difference between the foolish virgins and the wise ones was that the wise ones stayed prepared! How many women-in-waiting nowadays try to borrow oil from their sisters simply because they are not prepared? In other words, many women try to connect to any and every woman they see walking in holiness and trusting God for their husbands. They think by connecting to those women that they will share in their oil and in their testimonies. No! God requires that we all be ready and this is a lesson the foolish virgins had to learn the hard way.

Your oil is your anointing and it is tied to your purpose and your ministry. Have you seen your own oil? What is it that you were placed in the realm of the earth to do? Your oil is important to you. You don't need it to prepare for your husband; you need it to complete your assignment on earth. A lot of women want to get their husbands before they get their identities, but God prefers to give us our identities first. That way, we don't reject our God-given identities for our roles as wives. Believe it or not, this is easy to do. It's easy to become so comfortable being some man's wife that you don't want to venture out to do anything else. Being your husband's wife is not the most important role you'll have in this life. Your most important role is being a servant of the Most High God.

The quickest and easiest way to prepare for your God-appointed husband is by simply submitting your life and mind to God. You must commit to serving Him all the days of your life, and you can't just do this to get a husband. After all, God hears our words, but He compares them to what is in our hearts. If your words don't match the content and intent of your heart, you have lied to the Lord. That's why you shouldn't speak what you do not feel. Instead, spend this time asking the Lord to change you and make you a better servant and daughter to Him. Ask Him to teach you His ways, give you His heart and remove everything from you that is unlike Him. When you notice your life being shaken up, don't fret. Sometimes, God sifts away from us the things and the people that keep us from Him. What I do nowadays is... anytime my life is being disrupted by a sifting, in the midst of my tears, I say to the Lord, "God, let your will be done." I try to make sure that I'm not resisting Him in any way and I let go of anything and anyone He tells me to release. I'm not going to fight a fight that I cannot win, plus, I know that if God is removing something or someone from my life, it is for my own good and His glory.

Below are 20 things you can do to prepare for your God-ordained husband:

1. **Get closer to God.** Start a daily prayer life and get serious about your relationship with God.

2. **Denounce Satan and all of his works.** This includes watching reality television, listening to music that promotes sin, hanging out with your ungodly friends, gossiping, backbiting, slandering others, etc.

3. **Disassociate from ungodly people.** This includes friends, family members and church members. Ask the Lord to remove the people from your life that He does not want in it. Once you pray this prayer, you will notice that people will start distancing themselves from you. One of the most common things I hear people who've prayed this prayer say is that their phones became silent. They forgot that they had prayed for God to remove the wrong people from their lives. Many of them went out

and reconnected with the people
God was trying to disconnect them
from. Stay disconnected from them!
God never removes anything or
anyone from your life unless He has
better in store for you.

4. **Ask the Lord to connect you to the people He's assigned you to.** Godly connections are just as important as Godly disconnections. Some people hold the pieces of the puzzle that God has assigned you to put together. The amazing part is... many of the people who hold the pieces aren't people you'd ordinarily surround yourself with. That's because we tend to surround ourselves with people who are like us, but God is calling us to new mindsets, and therefore, new connections.

5. **Become more organized.** You may be an organized woman, but there is

always room for improvement. Learn to be more organized. Start with cleaning up cluttered areas of your home and purchasing household items that would serve to help you become more organized.

6. **Ask yourself what flaws you have that would challenge the very fabric of your marriage, and then, seek to overcome them.** One of my flaws is that I get overwhelmed when I'm surrounded by people. I'm introverted and I love the peace and quiet of my own home. Because of this, I often avoid social gatherings. I hate to feel crowded, and anytime I do feel crowded, I get snippy. In other words, I sometimes behave like a cornered Chihuahua. I had to come to the realization that my husband may be a social butterfly, and I don't want to embarrass him by being the snippy, stressed woman in the corner

of a social gathering who's obviously ready to go home. So, I had to get out more and put myself in situations that I'm ordinarily uncomfortable with.

7. **Learn to cook more dishes or learn to cook... period.** Cooking is intimate. It is almost like making love to your husband's tastebuds. Having been married, I have to tell you that there is no lower feeling than to have your husband look forward to eating someone else's food. I've always known how to cook, but when my first husband told me that he couldn't wait to go to his aunt's house to get one of her pecan pies, I felt like a loser. I immediately went to the store, got the ingredients for pecan pie and taught myself to cook them. In today's day and age, it's amazing for me to meet women who say that they don't know how to cook, but

that's not a major problem because you can learn to cook. What amazes me is when a woman clearly doesn't want to learn. Instead, she wants a husband who can either cook or who is content with eating chicken noodles and hot dogs for the rest of his life. Love makes you want to come outside of your comfort zone and do something for other people, even when you don't feel like doing it. Love your husband enough to want to cook for him. Don't have him looking forward to eating out everyday or eating at someone else's house.

8. **Practice patience and embrace long-suffering.** I know that the man God sends is a man after His own heart, but you have to know that he is still human. He is going to make mistakes. He is going to offend you. There will be days when the word

"divorce" will fly through your mind, and maybe even out of your mouth. That's why you need patience and long-suffering to stay married. Anybody can get married, but it takes patience, love and a forgiving heart to stay married. Long-suffering is a fruit of the Holy Spirit, and you need it for your marriage to survive. Ask for it by name.

9. **Entrepreneurs often create business plans. Create a life plan for yourself and seek to become a better daughter to God and an all-around person.** What can you do to please God more? Who can you help? Buy yourself a small notebook or planner and just jot down some ideas as to what you can do to bring a smile to God's beautiful face everyday.

10. **Clean up or build your credit.** Order your credit report and start paying off bills a little at a time. If you can pay

them off, pay them off.

11. **Stay out of debt.** I live by the rule that if I can't afford to buy it with cash, it's not my season to have it. If you can't afford a couch, sit on whatever you can afford. Instead of paying monthly notes on furniture, put that money away and buy your furniture one piece at a time. The point is... stay out of debt. Women in debt almost always give themselves to the first Ishmael who appears to be financially sound. Avoid debt.

12. **Learn to become financially dependent on God so that you will not depend on your husband.** Go back to school, start a new career or tap into your God-given talents. There is much you can learn to do... even from within the comfort of your own home. Make up your mind to become a blessing to the kingdom of God and a blessing to your husband.

13.Confront your fears and overcome them. When I was married the second time, I lived in Florida where Anole lizards are common. Every few months, a lizard would get into the apartment my ex and I were living in, and I would panic until he found and removed it or killed it. When we started going through a divorce, I had no choice but to confront my fears. A lizard got into my living room, and even though there may have been a more humane way to remove it, I didn't know of one, so I overkilled it. I had to also start confronting spiders once I moved to Georgia. As a woman living alone, I couldn't rush out of the house in my pajamas and ask the first man I saw to rescue me from the eight-legged monsters who kept coming in my apartment. I had to kill them myself. In addition to our fear of insects, we must confront other fears as well. For example, I've come across many women who are afraid to get on an airplane or a cruise ship. I've met women who are afraid of speaking in public. There are many fears that we often find ourselves bound by, but in your season of singleness, seek to overcome those fears. Don't just live with them and don't sit around and brag about them. Overcome them.

14. **Forgive everyone who's wronged you.** The truth is... some people don't deserve your forgiveness, but give it to them anyway. After all, you don't deserve God's forgiveness, but He sent Christ to die for your sins anyway. We are often challenged to do for others what Christ has done for us, and many of us fail in the area of love. Don't throw away your blessings just to sit around and be mad at someone. People are

imperfect creatures, and yes, some people set out to hurt others, but God will deal with them. Your focus ought to be on doing whatever it is that God has assigned you to do and let God deal with everything and everyone else. I wouldn't give the devil the satisfaction of me being mad at anyone. Instead, I chose love (and you should too) because God is love. Let bygones be bygones and keep your eyes on the prize: an eternity with the King of kings and Lord of lords.

15. **End all communications with every Ishmael who comes into your life the moment you realize they are Ishmaels!** An ex of mine attempted to reenter my life, and even though I liked talking with him, I had to end my communications with him. I realized that he was not my God-appointed husband, and he was truly

an Ishmael because he looked and
sounded like the promised man. My
flesh didn't want to end our
communications because I loved
being flattered and I loved being
pursued, but I couldn't pretend that I
didn't know better. I knew that he
would be a husband-blocker and I
didn't want him in my husband's way,
so I ended all communications after
three days. I watched one of my
closest friends shut every Ishmael-
access door the minute she realized
they weren't her husbands, and I
learned the importance of
immediately slamming doors from
her. The battle of the flesh against
the spirit was real. My flesh wanted
to entertain the ex, even though he
wasn't the God-sent one.
Nevertheless, I had to practice what I
preached or shut up and sit down.
Stop entertaining Ishmaels. I see so

many women doing this, and of
course, they'll justify their behaviors
by saying they are attempting to win
their exes' souls for the Lord. It's a
lie. They are trying to win their exes'
back to themselves, all the while,
using the name of the Lord to justify
their connections. Some of them
don't want the exes back. They
simply like being pursued and
flattered, much like I did. But to
continue communicating with an
Ishmael is not only selfish, but it
could prove to be dangerous. The
minute you realize a man is not your
God-appointed husband, you need to
end all communications with him...
pronto!

16. **Clean up your vocabulary.** Whether
you're cursing, speaking word curses,
gossiping, slandering or just releasing
negative words into the atmosphere,
you need to clean up your

vocabulary. You will have whatever you say, and that's why you need to speak what you want to manifest in your life. To remove a word from your vocabulary, you must first become aware of it, and after that, anytime you speak it, correct it.

17. **Guard the doors of your heart and house.** Stop allowing the enemy to have access to your heart through music, television and bad connections. Stop entertaining the flesh with foolishness and start building your spirit man with godly music, television and connections. Throw away every CD you have that promotes sin and unholy living. You have to change your mind on purpose before you can better understand your purpose.

18. **Practice interceding for others, including your God-appointed husband.** Intercession is a big part of

ministry and it helps us to become less selfish and more loving. Start praying for others more. Look for opportunities to pray for others. Your goal is to become more like God and less like the you you've gotten comfortable with.

19. **Court yourself.** Take yourself out to eat, go to the movies by yourself and treat yourself to the time of your life often. Don't wait for a man to do for you what God has given you the ability to do for yourself. A lot of women end up with the wrong men because their Ishmaels spent ten dollars more on them than they were willing to spend on themselves. In other words, the wrong men treated them better than they'd ever treated themselves, so they mistook them for good men. Get dressed up and court yourself! Treat yourself so well that it'll be hard for any man to compete

with. Understand that the more you
require of yourself, the higher the
standard you'll set for yourself. Don't
just court yourself, let God court you.
Spend time with Him. Go out on a
picnic with you and the Lord. Open
your Bible and meet the Lord on the
beach. Go to the park and walk with
the Lord. What you're doing is
learning that you can be happy and
single while preparing for your God-
appointed husband. Women who
don't do anything for themselves
often become overly anxious and end
up marrying the wrong men.

20. **Commit or recommit to God that
you will wait and prepare for the
one He's chosen, and you will not
choose your own husband anymore.**
Waiting for the promised man is not
just something we participate in; it
has to be a lifestyle. You are to
intentionally prepare for him while

you anticipate his arrival. Live a life
of expectancy. Look at your life and
seek ways to make it better.
Surround yourself with positive
people and rid your life of negative
influences. Everyday that you wake
up is a day that God expects to hear
from you. Start your day by sending
up a new commitment to heaven.
Recommit to preparing for your God-
ordained husband each and everyday
that you live.

There are many things you can do to
prepare for your God-assigned husband.
You know your own struggles and you know
your own strengths. Talk to the Lord about
your struggles and if He instructs you to do
so, use your strengths to overcome your
weaknesses. Spend this time with God,
seeking His heart all the more. Don't spend
your single season chasing up behind the
idea of marriage. Spend your single season

getting closer to the Lord. The closer you get to God, the closer you'll get to being found by your husband. The distance between you and your husband is the same distance between you and God. You can't put a man before God, so repent of all of your idolatrous ways today and recommit yourself to the Lord.

Waiting for the Promised Man

We all know the story of Moses and how God used him to free the Jews from Egypt. Moses had been taken in by Pharaoh's daughter when he was an infant. He'd been raised in the lap of luxury, but little did he know that his position inside the royal palace had been preordained by God. God allowed Moses to be taken in by Pharaoh's daughter because He planned to use him to free the Jews.

One day, Moses risked it all by killing an Egyptian soldier because he witnessed the soldier beating a Hebrew man. He looked around to ensure that he wouldn't be seen before he killed the man, but somehow, the news got out anyway. The next day, when Moses tried to stop two Hebrew men from fighting one another, one of the men asked him if he was going to kill them the same way he killed the Egyptian soldier the previous day. That's when Moses realized that his secret was out. After Pharaoh found out what Moses had done, he sought to kill Moses, so Moses had to go into hiding in a place called Midian.

After the king of Egypt died, Moses had a supernatural encounter. He saw a burning bush, but to his surprise, the bush was not consumed with the fire. He went closer to the bush to observe it, and that's when the Lord began to instruct him. The Lord told him that He was going to send him to Egypt to free the Israelites. Of course, Moses was afraid and he questioned God about his assignment. Nevertheless, he decided to obey God and he went back to Egypt to confront Pharaoh.

As the story goes on, it tells us about the

signs and wonders that God performed right in front of Pharaoh, but Pharaoh's heart was hardened by God, so he refused to let the Jews go free. Eventually, Pharaoh did release the Jews because of the many plagues and catastrophes that came upon Egypt. However, after the Jews were free, Pharaoh immediately regretted his decision and decided to bring them back into captivity. The Jews were officially on the run, and they eventually came to the Red Sea, where God would perform His greatest miracle before them. The Lord parted the Red Sea and let the Jews cross over on the dry land, but when Pharaoh and his chariots tried to pursue the Jews, the Lord released the sea and Pharaoh, along with his soldiers, perished.

The Jews had witnessed firsthand the sovereign power of God. Moses led them to the Desert of Sin, where the bible tells us that they grumbled and complained about

Moses and Aaron. Aaron was Moses's
brother, and he served as his brother's
spokesman because Moses had a speech
impediment. In today's terms, Aaron was
pretty much Moses's assistant or right-hand
man. The Jews complained because they
were in a process that they did not want to
endure. They didn't want to go through the
desert and the wilderness to get to their
promised land. Instead, they wanted to
skip the process and go straight into their
blessings. After all, they'd seen God work,
so they knew that He could supernaturally
bring them out of the desert and the dry
places and take them directly into the land
flowing with milk and honey... the land He'd
spoken of. Nevertheless, it is clear that
they did not understand God. They didn't
understand that there was (and still is) a
process that they had to endure before they
reached the promises of God.

In their complaining, the Jews repeatedly

said that they wished they hadn't left their bondage in Egypt. After all, they'd gotten comfortable in bondage. They knew that they would eat every day and they knew around what time they would eat. Even though they were praying and crying out to God while in Egypt, they'd become content with their bondage. This is the state of many in the church today.

It is not uncommon to come across a woman who's spent her entire life in and out of ungodly relationships because of the mental bondage she was once enslaved to. She was repeatedly used, mistreated and abandoned, and eventually, she cried out to God to be delivered from her mindset. She petitioned heaven, asking for a husband or her God-appointed husband, but she didn't realize that there was a process she had to go through before she could reach her promised man. While going through this process, she found that God was stripping her of old mindsets, old friends and many of the things she'd grown accustomed to in her bondage. Frustrated with God, she murmured and complained about Him and the people He sent into her life to help her. She looked back at her years of bondage and realized that even though she had been mistreated and mishandled by many men, she, at least, had a man. Because of this, many women have perished in the desert of their sin because they refused to trust God. Faith without works is dead, therefore, people without faith are spiritually dead. After having practiced abstinence for a few months or years, many women-in-waiting have returned to their deserts of sin. That's because they never got delivered from their bondage. Instead, they tried to manipulate God into sending them husbands, not realizing that God is all-knowing. He knows the intent and content of our hearts. He knows our thoughts and He knows our plans. He knows everything there is to know about us because He is the Creator and we are His creations.

We've all been in the desert of sin at some point in our lives, and the majority of us have tried to fornicate our way into our blessings. We wanted to be our husbands' crowns, even when we didn't treasure ourselves. We wanted to be our husbands' help meets, even though we didn't have the wisdom, knowledge or the understanding to help the man of God if we had known him. We wanted to be our husbands' "good things", even though our hearts weren't good. We were selfishly grafted into religion, not knowing that God was calling us out of our wildernesses and into true freedom. Everyone of us had a "type" in relation to men because we didn't know that we were simply attracted to certain types of spirits, better known as familiar spirits. We went into the churches, hoping to catch some man's attention, but because

we were not yet free, we found our "types"
in the churches. We kept getting caught up
in the same trap set by different men, but
we were sure that our sin would pay off
someday. It didn't. God has freed us from
bondage, but we preferred our bondage
over the wait because in bondage, we were
rarely ever single. But when we were trying
to wait for the promised man, we were not
only single, but God had sent many of our
friends and family members away from us.

During the journey to the promised man,
many women fall and return to the
bondage they once complained about. One
by one, we watched as our sisters fell,
secretly wondering if we would make it.
The closer to him we got, the longer the
journey appeared. There were times when
we thought we were a few feet away from
our blessings, only to discover that the path
we were on was about to fork off and we'd
have to choose between the righteous path

and the short path. We wanted to stop and just accept one of the men we'd passed along the way; after all, the closer we got to God, the harder it became to walk past the Ishmaels Satan sent our way. That's when we learned that Satan fights dirty. At one point in our journeys, he was sending the normal day-to-day Ishmaels after us, but the further we got into our journeys, the more attention Satan paid to detail before releasing another Ishmael to intercept us. After a while, some of the Ishmaels who came our way were *almost* irresistible, but the wise women had enough oil to see who they were and pass them by. The foolish women hadn't brought enough oil, and in the dark, Ishmael looks just like Isaac. Some of them realized that the men pursuing them were Ishmaels, but because they'd been in the desert of sin for so long, they were too thirsty to resist them. One-by-one, our sisters fell and day-by-day our faith was tested at a whole new level. Why was it so hard to be found by the God-appointed husband when it was once so easy to get a man?

Eventually, the sand was gone and the women who'd survived the journey turned around and realized that many of their sisters had fallen along the way. They weren't bruised, scarred or injured from the journey, but they were weary. Nevertheless, when they met their promised men, they better understood why they had to prepare for them. They understood why they had to labor for them. Their character had been built during the wait. Many of them had started their journeys as one woman, only to have God change the very fabric of their DNA along the way.

Their promised men stepped forward to claim them, but it was at that moment that they realized how much God had changed them during their journeys. They were excited to be found by their God-appointed husbands, but they were no longer desperate to be found by them. After they were found and produced the evidence of their faith, many of them were handed Moses's assignment and sent back into Egypt to help free their sisters. This time, their husbands accompanied them along the way, and they were able to successfully bring many women back to Christ and help them to position themselves to be found. Make no mistake about it... this journey isn't about being found by some man who's been dubbed as your God-appointed husband. For God, this journey is about dying to the flesh and finding our way back to Him. After all, too many women have made an idol out of marriage, and God will not hand you a man to worship and adore! When God positions us to be found, it will be because we found Him and we learned to put Him first in our lives.

I hear so many women talking about how they are worth waiting for, but not too many of them realize that their God-appointed husbands are worth waiting for as well. That's because many of God's daughters haven't forgiven the men of their past. It goes without saying that God won't release your husband to you if you have not released one or more of the men from your past.

I was God's stubborn, impatient daughter (like most women), and because of my refusal to wait on God, I found myself in two marriages that the enemy designed to destroy me. After having been physically and verbally abused, cheated on repeatedly, scammed, lied to, lied on and mistreated, I found myself in a worse place than the women who were single and waiting. They, at least, had hope, but I felt hopeless. I wasn't a victim of the men I'd chosen for myself. I was a victim of my own lack of knowledge and my own rebellion. That's why I don't speak reproachfully about them. I testify about what I've gone through, but I try to be careful with my words because they are souls too and God loves them. Not only have I forgiven them, but I understand the choices they made over the course of our marriages, even though their choices hurt me. First and foremost, their choices hurt God, so I couldn't put myself first in line and claim to be a victim. I was a lost soul who'd met two lost souls. I found my way out through the grace of God, but when we parted ways, they were still lost. Because of this, I'll testify about what I've gone through, but only when it's necessary. Think of it this way... You and your best friend were lost on a mountaintop. There was no food and the clothing you were both wearing was too thin to protect you from the below zero weather. To survive, both of you ate the carcasses of whatever dead animals you found, regardless of what conditions they were in. You were both delirious, had sleepless nights and fought over the simplest things.

One day, you decided to find your way back to civilization, but your friend chose to stay behind. She was angry with you for even thinking about leaving her behind. She was angry with you for not being content with the lives you were both sharing. She was angry with you for wanting better, so before you left, she did everything in her power to hurt you. She viciously attacked you, refused to let you eat and she spoke all manners of evil about you. Despite what she's done, you left anyway, but the scars she inflicted on you made your journey a lot harder than it should have been.

After weeks descending the mountain and going through the wilderness, you find your way back to civilization, and you've got a testimony to share. People flock around you to hear about your experiences and many hikers and backpackers take notes, hoping that they don't find themselves in your old shoes. You've got a choice to make regarding your old friend. You can tell everybody how wicked she was towards you and say that she's still stranded on the mountaintop because of how she treated you, or you can send help. I think so many of us get caught up in who did what to us that we forget that another soul needs help. We forget that we were once lost when we come across lost souls, but through the grace of God, we found our way back to Christ. The point here is clear. We've got to forgive those who've hurt us, otherwise, we will not meet the men we've been praying for. Know this: When you're still mad at one man, you're going to take it out on every man who gets as close to you as that man once was.

When I started going through the second divorce, I was truly a woman after God's own heart. I carefully and consciously ministered to myself as I went through every step of the divorce and every emotion that arose during the divorce process. I told myself that I was going to forgive my ex. I told myself that I was going to pray for my ex. I told myself that I was going to be okay; I would survive what I was going through. And God confirmed every word that I spoke, and when I asked Him to make these things happen, He did. While we were divorcing, my ex stopped by my apartment to drop off a package, and it was then that I was able to lead him through the sinner's prayer. I'd forgiven him, and even though I was hurt about all that was going on, I learned to separate my pain from God's love. God loved him. He was still lost and He needed guidance. He didn't deserve to go to Hell because of what he'd done to me. He deserved another chance, just as

God had given me another chance. I tell
this story to help you to understand the
importance of releasing the old men to
receive the promised man. Forgiveness is a
choice! Yes, I was angry and hurt, but in the
midst of my pain, I chose to forgive.

Many women-in-waiting are still angry with
one or more of the men from their pasts,
but instead of confronting their unforgiving
hearts, they are praying to God to send
them husbands. Here's the thing: God is a
God who blesses His children. He's not
going to send a faithful, God-fearing man
who's been trusting Him for his wife to an
unfaithful, unforgiving woman who wants
to idolize him. That's like winning first place
in a race, only to be rewarded with a
lashing. Sometimes, the wilderness that a
woman is in is the desert of unforgiveness.
She says she's forgiven the men from her
past, but she's not being honest with
herself or others. How can you tell if you're

still walking in unforgiveness? The Bible tells us that the heart knows its own bitterness. Ask yourself these few questions and be completely honest with yourself:

- Do you want your ex to fail?
- Do you think your ex still owes you an apology?
- Do you still get angry when you think about what the ex took you through?
- Do you still want revenge on your ex?
- Do you look forward to the day when you can pass by your ex with a man who's better than him?
- Do you compare yourself to your ex's current lover?

If you've answered "yes" to any of the above questions, you are still in or battling unforgiveness. You cannot get to the promised man if you're still mad at the impostor. You can't wake up and decide that you have forgiven someone.

Forgiveness is a seed of will that eventually grows up to bear fruit. The evidence isn't always in your words; it is often found in your actions. It starts off as a thought, graduates into a prayer, and when you refuse to change your mind about it, it eventually becomes the condition of your heart, or better yet, an answered prayer.

Again, waiting is a passive word, whereas, preparing is an action word. A wife-in-waiting is not sitting around and counting down the days until she arrives at her promised land. Her wait is not intentional, meaning, it's not something she works at or works against. She is a woman who is actively pursuing the heart of God. This means that she's letting go of the things and the people God wants her to be free of. She has chosen to forgive the men in her past because God blessed her to understand why those men could not accompany her into the future. It wasn't their fault. They were simply not assigned to her, and when God sent those men away from her, He was simply delivering her from them. Because of this, rather than exposing what embarrassing things they'd done while on the mountain, she should pray that God helps them to get off the mountain. Testimonies are designed to help others, not bash them.

I speak on forgiveness because a lot of you have not forgiven your exes or the people who've hurt you. And you're crying out to God time and time again, wondering why He hasn't sent the promised man to you yet. He wants you to release the people you're holding in your heart. We can all justify stewing in unforgiveness because just like you, we've all had people to do some pretty foul things to us, but we're still here so their weapons formed did not prosper. It is better to focus on what God brought you through than it is to focus on what people took you through; that way, you give Him the glory. My story is designed to help others; nothing more, nothing less. Your story is designed to help others; nothing more, nothing less.

Waiting for the promised man is not always fun. There will be times when you'll want to be held, romanced, loved on, kissed, complimented, danced with or comforted. There will be times when you'll want your husband's strong, loving arms wrapped around you. Rainy days will come and you'll want to spend those days lying next to your husband. Sunny days will come and you'll want to spend those days at the beach with your husband. Cold days will come and you'll want to spend those days in the arms of your husband. Those desires are your human side crying out for attention, but don't starve your spirit to feed your flesh. Spend that time with the Lord. When rainy days come, lie in the bed and talk with the

Lord. When sunny days come, go to the beach and spend that time with the Lord. When cold days come, let the Lord wrap His loving arms around you. Acknowledge His presence, even when you don't feel it. The more you feed your spirit man, the stronger your spirit will become against your flesh. Before long, waiting for the promised man won't be so difficult. Before long, you will know the love of God and it won't be so easy to take it for granted.

Understand that your past was your Egypt. God has brought you out; don't go back to it. Don't perish in the wilderness because of impatience. Simply trust God and let Him do what He's trying to do with you. Father knows best! Your promised man will come to you if you don't give up. Your promised man will find you if you don't come out of hiding to be with another man. Your promised man is more than a prayer away; he's needs you to trust God, obey God and serve God with all of your might so that you can transition from being a woman-in-waiting into a wife-in-waiting. In your single season, God will give you manna to get through each day. This manna is the wisdom of God that you'll need to sustain you. If you are simply following a bunch of singles' ministries, but you are not partaking of the Word of God, you are rejecting your manna. Singles' ministries are designed to encourage you, but they cannot sustain you. You need the Word of God, raw and uncut. That is your manna.

Today, decide that you will no longer be a woman-in-waiting, but you'll be a woman pursuing the heart of God with everything in you. If God can deliver me from the strongmen that once held me captive; the strongmen that had me thinking I couldn't live without being in a relationship with some man, I know that He can deliver you. My struggles led me into some dark places, but when God brought me out of them, I committed to Him and myself to go back to Egypt and lead back every last one of my sisters who heard God's voice in me and wanted to find their way to freedom. God delivered me. He healed and restored me, and then, He made me better than content as a single wife-in-waiting. I rejoice everyday, knowing that my appointed man of God will find me in submission to God.

God is extending an invitation to you to come back to Him. This invitation doesn't require that you be perfect; it is an invitation to start your journey out of Egypt and make your way towards the place that's better than the heart of the promised man... it is the heart of God. Reach out with your heart and commit to taking this journey. It won't be easy because flesh has no inheritance with God, so your flesh is going to die along the way. Understand that when someone says that the flesh will die, they aren't saying that you, yourself will die. They are saying that God is going to crucify the lusts of the flesh, meaning, everything that leads you away from God will be put to death. It sounds difficult, but it isn't as hard as we make it out to be. Let God be God in your life. Trust Him to lead you out of bondage; do not trust yourself. Talk to the Lord about every struggle you have, even those struggles you aren't sure you're ready to part with. God will change your mind; He will change your heart. Come out of the desert of sin and tear down the comfort zones that have held you in bondage. Understand that life is nothing but a continuous shifting and tearing down of comfort zones, and those who are willing to let God shake up their lives are the ones who'll find themselves on steady ground.

Your husband is out there somewhere, waiting to find you... or maybe he's still in his very own desert of sin. However, if God

called the two of you together, no devil,
evil, power or principality will be able to
keep the two of you apart. You simply need
to get into position so you can start
interceding on the behalf of your God-
appointed husband.

Your journey to the promised man isn't as
long and as difficult as the enemy would
have you believe. He knows that the
journey is designed to kill those parts of
your flesh that he's been using against you.
This means he will lose his power to
persuade you and, of course, he doesn't
want that. Your journey to the promised
man requires that you give yourself over to
God and you learn to trust Him with every
facet of your being. I took the journey, and
I can tell you from where I stand, I'm glad
that I did. I lost a lot along the way, but I'm
thankful nonetheless because God has
greater in store for me. If He doesn't do
anything else for me, He has already proven

Himself to be a great, faithful and loving God... a God who rewards the faithful at heart and protects His own.

When Satan realized that I wasn't going to give up and that I was going all the way, He attacked me viciously. He attacked my finances repeatedly; he attacked my peace, and then, he sent an Ishmael after me. When I rejected the Ishmael, he turned up the heat on his attack, but I wasn't going to give up, give in or make a deal with the devil. I continued to trust God through it all, and God brought me through. These are not the types of things that happen when you are preparing for your God-ordained husband; these are the things that happen when you are PREPARED for your God-ordained husband. You see, Satan is stupid enough to tell you where you are in your wait, if you'll only stop crying and complaining and pay attention to the temperature of the attack. It'll let you know what season you're in.

Prepare for the promised man; he's coming if you're willing to let God bring you out of the desert of sin, through the wilderness and into His perfect will. God has a plan for you. There will be times when it feels like God has forgotten you, but He hasn't. Like a father with a toddler, He will sometimes stand just a few feet away from you and extend His hands to you. You're used to Him carrying you, but He's saying that you have the ability to stand on your own and He's teaching you to walk on your own. During this time, you may fall and the fall does hurt, but all God wants you to do is get back up and keep on heading towards His opened arms. He wants you to stand for Him so you won't fall for the lies of the enemy. I've seen many sisters fall along the way... some of them were powerful women in ministry, but somehow, the enemy managed to convince them that sin would produce a better and quicker blessing than obedience would. <u>Satan is a liar and we must remember this</u>. Those women fell, but they forgot one thing: Satan hates them. Some of them went into blatant witchcraft, while others, found themselves battling for their lives. This isn't to scare you; it's to remind you that Satan doesn't have a blessing with your name on it. He has a coffin with your name on it, but to get you in it, he will lie to you and send one man after the other to derail, distract and destroy you. God, on the other hand, wants to bless and prosper you. He has no evil thoughts concerning you. He is not mad at you and He is not seeking to punish you. He loves you and He wants you to turn away from your sin and to seek His face like never before. A man isn't the answer to your problems; God is. When you find yourself content with God, He will send the promised man to find you, and he won't find you in desperation, nor will he find you

in the desert of sin. He will find you in a
state of peace, prosperity and joy... a place
where God has proven Himself to you and
demonstrated His majesty to you.

Jeremiah 29:11-14 (ESV): For I know the
plans I have for you, declares the Lord,
plans for welfare and not for evil, after
courting his now fiance for three years to
give you a future and a hope. Then you will
call upon me and come and pray to me, and
I will hear you. You will seek me and find
me, when you seek me with all your heart.
I will be found by you, declares the Lord,
and I will restore your fortunes and gather
you from all the nations and all the places
where I have driven you, declares the Lord,
and I will bring you back to the place from
which I sent you into exile.